Searching for

A Christian Companion

Susan Hibbins

Copyright © Trustees for Methodist Church Purposes, 2005
Cover picture photo: © LiquidLibrary

British Library Cataloguing in Publication data

A catalogue record for this book is available
from the British Library

ISBN 1 85852 292 7

First published by Inspire
4 John Wesley Road
Werrington
Peterborough PE4 6ZP

Printed and bound in Great Britain by
Stanley L. Hunt (Printers) Ltd, Rushden

Contents

Foreword

As I write this Foreword, the people of London are reeling from four bomb attacks which have killed more than 50 and injured hundreds more. Suicide bombers in Iraq and elsewhere continue their deadly missions. Wars and civil conflicts in other countries cause hunger, disease and despair. In our own society there is often an atmosphere of unease, even fear; greater aggression results in shorter tempers and increasing violence. To talk about searching for peace in all this might seem a hopeless task. Where do we start looking?

Christians speak of the peace of God that 'passes understanding' – a peace that endures even in the midst of conflict, in difficult circumstances and personal trials that threaten to overwhelm us and leave us feeling anything but peaceful. Is it realistic to talk about peace in our hearts when everything around us is threatening to fall apart? Or is it heartless, callous, unfeeling? Again, where do we look for such peace?

The articles in this year's *Christian Companion* try to answer some of these questions. Some of the authors find glimpses of peace in nature, in moments when God seems to draw nearer in the sights and sounds of his creation. Cecily Taylor speaks of 'a valley of green peacefulness' in which she finds an unchanging wisdom and balm for her soul. Michaela Youngson recounts moments of peace, some fleeting, in which

God's peace is apparent in everyday events and encounters. In the article 'Searching through the wreckage', Margaret Cundiff finds a 'fragile' peace when she is able to put her trust in Jesus Christ, even when it sometimes seems impossible to do so. Kenneth Greet puts forward a 'peacemaker's quadrilateral', suggesting ways in which people can work to prevent further wars.

A number of articles consider the search for peace in our troubled world, and find glimmers of hope in unlikely places. Andrew White's article on the Alexandria Peace Process shows what can be achieved when people try to put aside long-held divisions and begin to talk to one another. It may not bring instant results, but if a dialogue can at least begin it can bring a hope for peace. John Morrow, reflecting on the past conflicts of Northern Ireland, finds the beginnings of reconciliation in small acts of trust, in people standing together in solidarity against the effects of violence and hatred. Peter Selby and Sheila O'Hara long for the peace that greater economic opportunity and justice would bring to the world's poorest nations.

Most Christians are troubled when they find a lack of peace within the Church. In the place where the peace of God should be paramount it is often absent, and relationships can be strained and anything but loving. Too much change too quickly is sometimes given as the cause of arguments in churches, but here Peter Middlemiss feels that we can retain our serenity if we accept that the nature of God is about change – and yet remains the same in his love and care for us. Conflict in the Church is the theme of Harriet Harris' article, specifically the heartache and conflict brought about by the debate surrounding human sexuality. In our search for peace, she maintains, we should not compromise and try to pretend that conflict does not exist: instead we should try our best to accept others within the love of Christ, even though we cannot always agree with one another.

David Painter reinforces this view, asserting that when we exchange the Peace within our church services, we both receive and give something of Christ. And receiving and giving is another main theme of *Searching for Peace*. The 'deep peace' we receive in our hearts from God, as Michael Thompson points out, it is to be shared, so that we ourselves become messengers of peace.

Perhaps that is the clue to bringing peace to our world. If we look only at the big picture we despair, but individually we can spread peace to the next person, and the next, and the next. In the words of Joyce Rupp:

> One single candle lights a little dark place.
> Many candles light a world full of people
> Desperately in need of each other's glow.
> Each lone light makes us stronger
> When we all stand together.*

Susan Hibbins
Editor, *A Christian Companion*

*Joyce Rupp, *The Cosmic Dance,* Orbis Books, 2002.

Searching through the wreckage

Margaret Cundiff

Christmas 2004, and I was feeling completely at peace, and with good reason. After all the pre-Christmas rush and activity, everything was in order, nothing left to worry about. Gifts and turkey under wraps, all the last-minute preparations done and dusted. The midnight celebration of Holy Communion had been a foretaste of heaven, and those words 'with angels and archangels, and all the company of heaven' had been to us all an affirmation of being part of the Church, the body of Christ, on earth and in heaven. We had almost lifted the roof as we sang our way into Christmas Day with the hymn:

> Hark! The herald angels sing
> Glory to the new-born King.
> Peace on earth, and mercy mild,
> God and sinners reconciled.

Peacefully and joyfully into Christmas, and the prospect also of a few days relaxing with the family, time just to be, to enjoy, to share together.

Within hours my peace, our peace, the world's fragile peace was shattered by a tidal wave in Asia, bringing destruction, devastation and death in its wake, taking lives, property and hope from an enormous area; and all we could do was watch on our TV screens the horror unfolding. The Christmas sense of peace which had been so beautiful and secure on Christmas Day was dashed by the events of Boxing Day and the days following, as we scrabbled around, trying to make sense of what was happening, while a new word, 'tsunami', began to dominate our lives and our thinking.

Yet horror and hopelessness turned to activity, as the world reacted by giving on a scale never known before. Aid and offers of help flooded in from every part of the world, and the expression 'One World' became no longer a slogan or sermon topic, but a living experience, and out of that experience the recognition of our responsibility for one another. Our peace had been battered and disturbed, and we were forced to challenge what we had taken for granted, and what we longed for: that peace, which seemed to be taken from us just as we thought we had it in our grasp.

But it is not just the effects of that tsunami that threaten our peace of mind, but mental and spiritual forces that threaten to overwhelm us. Paul, writing to the Christians in Ephesus 2,000 years ago, put it like this: 'For our struggle is not against enemies of blood and flesh, but against the rulers, against the authorities, against the cosmic powers of this present darkness, against the spiritual forces of evil in the heavenly places' (Ephesians 6.12). These are the disturbers of our peace in the twenty-first century also.

Life was not easy for those first believers, nor is it for us today. There are so many forces at work which we have to contend with, and sometimes we may feel we are being overwhelmed. Yet we have all we need not just to survive, but to overcome, and be enabled to reach out to help, hold and encourage others too. As we open ourselves to receive God's peace into our hearts, our minds and our lives we will find that inner strength we need. The prophet Isaiah could affirm: 'Those of steadfast mind you keep in peace – in peace because they trust you' (Isaiah 26.3) just as the psalmist could say, 'I will both lie down and sleep in peace; for you alone, O LORD, make me lie down in safety' (Psalm 4.8). How often do we lie down and twist and turn with the world's problems and our own worries going round and round in our head; no wonder we cannot sleep. We need to find a way to trust God, to recognize that he is Lord of all, and that he will work out his good purpose.

It is that word 'trust' we find so difficult, isn't it? Do we feel sometimes that God is unconcerned or unable to help us? Maybe we feel we are not worth caring about or helping – who are we to presume on God's mercy? If you ever feel like that, remember Jesus. As we look at him, God's gift of love to you, me and the whole world, becoming one with us to bring us to new life and to fill us with his peace, how can we doubt him? Surely he is the answer to our doubts and questions, and it is as we trust him that we will know that inner peace, keeping us steady and secure however hard the storms rage, and however our fragile beings are battered.

I think of that time when Jesus asked his friends to take him across the lake, so that they could have some peace and quiet away from the demanding crowds. It should have been an easy trip, for four of them were professional fishermen, they were all used to handling boats in all weather, all circumstances; they knew the lake, they knew their trade. But a terrible storm blew up, and it seemed that their boat and all of them in it would be drowned. It was too much for them to handle. So where was Jesus when they needed him? Asleep, oblivious of their needs, of the danger. In desperation and fear they yelled, 'Teacher do you not care we are perishing?' Jesus spoke with authority to the elements, 'Peace, be still', and immediately peace came, the storm was stilled, the lake was quiet. Then Jesus spoke a gentle but firm rebuke to his friends, 'Why are you afraid? Have you still no faith?'

I know I need to hear and heed those words of Jesus. There are times when like Corporal Jones from *Dad's Army* I lose my confidence, and go round shouting, 'Don't panic, don't panic!' instead of calming down, and listening. We all panic at times, and feel out of our depth, and wonder what Jesus is doing, or if he is there at all. Remember his words, and remember too his command, 'Peace, be still!' Over and over again Jesus offered his friends his gift of peace, but how soon they forgot what he had given them, what was within them to know and use. After he was taken from them, put to death and buried in the tomb, they felt they would never know any peace. They locked themselves away, not only physically, but they locked into themselves their guilt, anxiety and despair. No way out, and all sense of peace had fled, had died, or so it seemed. Then the risen, living Lord broke through locked doors, locked hearts and minds, with the same message, the same offer. 'Peace be with you.' And they were filled with joy, with peace and with power.

Today the world tries frantically to find peace, make peace, impose peace. Leaders of the nations travel round the world attending councils and conferences, issuing statements, reports, even sending in troops to make peace. There are gatherings of the great and good; the Churches hold their synods and assemblies, and we try to do our bit in working for peace, but maybe again it is the Corporal Jones approach rather than the offer of Jesus, and no wonder we all fail, in spite of our best efforts and intentions. The peace that alone can transform the world, the Church, you and me is the peace of God, made known in Jesus. 'He [Jesus] is our peace.' He breaks down all barriers, overcomes all problems and sadness, and has overcome death itself. His peace is for here and now. Just stop and think about that, let it sink into your heart, your mind, your life. Receive his peace now, and keep on receiving it so it becomes part of you, and flows out from you to others. Become one of the peacemakers that Jesus calls 'blessed'. For we are blessed with the gift of peace, if we will accept it by faith and with joy. Searching for peace? No need to go on searching, it is here for us now: 'Peace be with you.' The peace of the Lord be always with you!

Now there was a great wind, so strong that it was splitting mountains and breaking rocks in pieces before the LORD, but the LORD was not in the wind; and after the wind an earthquake, but the LORD was not in the earthquake; and after the earthquake a fire, but the LORD was not in the fire; and after the fire a sound of sheer silence.

1 Kings 19.11-12

The Creator who brought order out of chaos,
give peace to you
The Saviour who stilled the raging storm,
give peace to you.
The Spirit who broods on the deeps,
give peace to you.

David Adam

Now I want you to think that in life troubles will come, which seem as if they never would pass away. The night and storm look as if they would last forever; but the calm and the morning cannot be stayed; the storm in its very nature is transient. The effort of nature, as that of the human heart, ever is to return to its repose, for God is peace.

George Macdonald

'Let the mountains be moved and the hills shake, my compassion towards thee stands immovable' (Isaiah 54.10). In the hours of weariness and discouragement, when the road seems long and one feels weighed down by one's misery, inadequacy and weakness, it is good to think of our Lord's immutable love, which nothing can discourage and which remains always ready to receive us ... And we know that the future is in the hands of him who loves us, and that he will be there always; that in the midst of the desert, all through the night, his hand will hold ours.

Dominican nun

At the heart of the cyclone tearing the sky
And flinging the clouds and the towers by,
Is a place of central calm:
So here in the roar of mortal things,
I have a place where my spirit sings,
In the hollow of God's Palm.

Edwin Markham

Help us, O Lord, to live one day at a time. Let your grace be sufficient for today. Let me not be anxious about tomorrow. Let me rest in the arms of your love in time and in eternity, blessed by your goodness, now and forever.

Corrie ten Boom

For a time will come when your innermost voice will speak to you, saying: 'This is my path; here I shall find peace. I will pursue this path, come what may.'

Grace Cooke

He leads us on by paths we did not know,
Upward he leads us, though our steps be slow,
Though oft we faint and falter on the way,
Though storms and darkness oft obscure the day,
    Yet when the clouds are gone,
    We know he leads us on.

He leads us on through all the unquiet years,
Past all our dreamland hopes, and doubts and fears,
He guides our steps through all the tangled maze
Of losses, sorrows, and o'erclouded days,
    We know his will is done,
    And still he leads us on.

N.L. Zinzendorf

Christ's life outwardly was one of the most troubled lives that was ever lived: tempest and tumult, tumult and tempest, the waves breaking over it all the time. But the inner life was a sea of glass. The great calm was always there.

Henry Drummond

He was speaking about the blessed life, the abundant life. How few had been far-visioned enough to claim that perfect life for their own. A life freed of fear and foreboding, freed of frets and suspicions, freed of the sweating greed for perishable things. This was the life he offered, a life of enduring peace in the midst of the world's clamours and confusions. Esther's sense yielded to it ... the Carpenter's peace invited her spirit. He was defining the terms of it now. Anyone could possess it. It was to be had for the asking, but one must seek for it, work for it; and, if need be, suffer for it. It was like living water, drawn from an ever-flowing stream. Once you had tasted of it, you would never be satisfied without it.

Lloyd C. Douglas

Grant that I may rest in thee above all things that
    can be desired,
    and let my heart may be at peace in thee.
·Thou art the true peace of the heart, thou
        its only rest;
        out of thee all things are irksome and restless.
In this very peace which is in thee, the one Supreme
        Eternal Good,
        I will sleep and take my rest.

Thomas à Kempis

Not as the world gives

David Painter

Oh, for a bit of peace!

Words such as these are frequently on the lips of the stressed-out executive, the tired commuter, the busy housewife or the parents of demanding children – indeed, we all say something like this from time to time. And we think we know what we mean when we do so; we mean that we wish we could sit still for a while, that we could be quiet, or that we could be left alone.

In a wider context, we understand peace to be the ending of war or conflict, which is presumably what most people have in mind when they pray for peace. Day by day and week by week we lay before God, for his healing, the seemingly intractable problems of the Middle East or Northern Ireland – to name but two of the world's obvious trouble spots – and pray that somehow, despite all the false starts, broken promises and betrayed hopes, men and women will stop fighting each other and will learn to live in peace and harmony.

Peace, then, conveys to most of us the notion of an absence of conflict, stress or noise, and in that sense is generally thought of as something eminently desirable but rarely achievable.

But is that what our Lord meant when, at his Last Supper with his disciples, he said, 'Peace I leave with you; my peace I give to you – *not as the world gives do I give to you*'? I am haunted by these words, for they seem to suggest that our fairly basic understanding of peace (such as I have outlined above) may not necessarily be the only understanding, but rather that our Lord's peace is paradoxically to be found, not in the absence of conflict, but at the heart of where conflict and opposition and struggle take place. And if our Lord's words at the Last Supper are puzzling, they are matched by his even more challenging assertion that 'I have not come to bring peace, but a sword. I have come to set a man against his father, and a daughter against her mother ... and one's foes will be members of one's own household' (Matthew 10.34-36). These words can actually give us hope in the Church, for they could suggest that so far from being embarrassed about disagreements in church circles when they take place, we should expect them to happen. More than that, we should see in such disagreements the working-out of our Lord's purpose for his Church and his world, for peace comes when people stop trying to avoid conflict, or to get round it, or to paper over the cracks, and instead face conflict honestly, learning to live with it, and – above all – holding in respect, trust and esteem those with whom they disagree. This peace is 'not as the world gives' – but it is, I believe, a peace that Christ longs to give us and show us if we will let him.

It scarcely needs to be said that to receive and reflect this kind of peace will nearly always require a change of heart. Human pride is a very powerful force, and it is often fear of loss of face or prestige which prevents us from loving our enemies (another of our Lord's uncomfortable commands). When we pray for Christ's peace we are really praying for the grace to be changed, to become 'unworldly' in the best sense of that word. This seems to me to be a more Christlike prayer than one which simply looks for conflict to end, for as long as human beings inhabit the earth conflict will not end, and reconciliation means not a state in which people necessarily agree with one another about any issue before them, but rather a willingness on the part of those who disagree – sometimes very profoundly – to accept one another as fellow human beings, and as brothers and sisters in Christ.

In a sermon which the Archbishop of Canterbury preached to the General Synod of the Church of England in July 2003 he referred to God's purpose, as set forth in the Letter to the Ephesians, to 'unite all things in Christ', and he made the following striking assertion.

> A New Testament Church is one in which unity is seen as vital precisely because it invites us to struggle for blessing as we wrestle with a stranger. If someone else stands with me claiming the promises of Christ, then, for St Paul, my first assumption must always be that in unity – in conversation and struggle, agreement, argument, shared praise – I shall receive from that person something of Christ.

'I shall receive from that person something of Christ.' Such an expectation may seem light years away from the mutual suspicion and intolerance which characterize so much debate and dialogue in the Church today. Many Christians seem to anticipate receiving 'something of Christ' only from those fellow Christians with whom they are in agreement, and who share their values and presuppositions. To expect to receive 'something of Christ' from those whom we find it hard to understand and harder still to like is surely what we are called and challenged to try to achieve, and the achieving of it will surely lead us to experience a peace which is 'not as the world gives'.

I wonder whether an honest seeking of this kind of peace may inform our thinking about the custom of exchanging the Peace – by means of a greeting, a handshake or an embrace – at the Eucharist. This custom was first introduced (or reintroduced) in the 1970s, and although it is still fiercely resisted by some congregations it is widely practised in most branches of the Church. Part of the unease which some people express about the practice could well stem from our English resistance to informality or 'mateyness', but there may be a deeper and more significant hurdle to be faced. The exchanging of the Peace can be done too easily and even too casually, and if this is the case there will be a danger of masking some real divisions within the congregation – divisions which need to be honestly faced if Christ's peace is to be real. Confession and absolution, the recognition of our failure to love and an openness to the kind of change to which I have referred earlier – all these need to be in place if the peace of Christ is to become a reality. More than that, a congregation capable of a real sharing of a real Peace is one in which the members dare to 'speak the truth in love' (Ephesians 4.15), and can thus, by looking each other in the eye and grasping each other's hands, convey something utterly different from the vapid cheerfulness that sometimes characterizes this section of the Liturgy.

Let the last word be with the Archbishop of Canterbury – from the sermon of his from which I have already quoted.

> Jesus arises to disturb the whole world's peace for the sake of the whole world's salvation, for the sake of unity between heaven and earth. To live in his peace, in his unity, is to live constantly in the presence of his call to be converted. It is to recognise the immense cost of a unity that truly brings differences into a shared praise, and to accept that it will cost us everything. The luxury of separation is really death; the pain of unity is really life for us, who are destined and appointed to live for the praise of his glory.

'I have said these things to you while I am still with you. But the Advocate, the Holy Spirit, whom the Father will send in my name, will teach you everything, and remind you of all that I have said to you. Peace I leave with you; my peace I give to you. I do not give to you as the world gives. Do not let your hearts be troubled, and do not let them be afraid. ... I have said these things to you so that my joy may be in you, and that your joy may be complete.'

John 14.25-27, 15.11

'Blessed are the peacemakers: for they shall be called the children of God.' The followers of Jesus have been called to peace. When he called them they found their peace, for he is their peace. But now they are told that they must not only have peace but make it. [Christ's] kingdom is one of peace, and the mutual greeting of his flock is the kiss of peace. His disciples keep the peace by choosing to endure suffering themselves rather than inflict it on others. They maintain fellowship where others would break it off. They renounce all self-assertion, and preserve a dignified silence in the face of hatred and wrong.

Dietrich Bonhoeffer

When you are proclaiming peace with your lips, be careful to have it even more fully in your heart.

Francis of Assisi

We all desperately want peace. ... That is why *shalom* is such an oft-repeated word. For, even as a simple greeting, it embodies deep yearning and solemn promise. So the ancient sage Hillel insisted that it is not enough to simply want peace, to hope for peace, even to pray for peace; he taught us to 'love peace and actively pursue peace'.

Wayne Dosick

Peace is the gift of God. Do you want peace? Go to God. Do you want peace in your families? ... If you do, live your religion, and the very peace of God will dwell and abide with you, for that is where peace comes from, and it doesn't dwell anywhere else.

John Taylor

Always keep God's peace and love among you, and when you have to seek guidance about your affairs, take great care to be of one mind. Live in mutual goodwill also with Christ's other servants, and do not despise Christians who come to you for hospitality, but see that you welcome them, give them accommodation, and send them on their way with friendship and kindness. Never think you are superior to other people who share your faith and way of life.

Cuthbert's last words, according to Bede

Whatever form the giving of the Peace may take – to turn and share the Peace is to make a new beginning on each occasion. It is a tacit acknowledgement of one's failures in relationship and action and a loving acceptance of the other person with all their gifts, inconsistencies and needs. ... To share the peace with a handclasp in this way can be the first step towards reconciliation if relationships are strained, or it can be a gesture of thanksgiving for all that is good and loving between people.

Ann Bird

Show us, good Lord,
>   the peace we should seek,
>   the peace we must give,
>   the peace we must keep,
>   the peace we must forgo,
>   and the peace you have
>   given us in Jesus our Lord.

Anonymous

We make a gesture of general reconciliation. It may be a mile away from love, but it is a step, a confession that we do wish to go there, and it is certainly kinder than no gesture at all.

J. Neville Ward

One of the crowd went up,
And knelt before the Paten and the Cup,
Received the Lord, returned in peace, and prayed
Close to my side; then in my heart I said:

'O Christ, in this man's life –
This stranger who is thine – in all his strife,
All his felicity, his good and ill,
In the assaulted stronghold of his will,

'I do confess thee here,
Alive within this life; I know thee near
Within this lonely conscience, closed away
Within this brother's solitary day.

'Christ in his unknown heart,
His intellect unknown – this love, this art,
This battle, and this peace, this destiny,
That I shall never know, look upon me!

'Christ in his numbered breath,
Christ in his beating heart and in his death,
Christ in his mystery! From that secret place
And from that separate dwelling, give me grace.'

Alice Meynell

Ssh now ...

Donald Macaskill

Ssh now.
Don't speak.
Don't utter even a sound,
but let your heart listen;
so that the breeze touches your breath
and the fragrance of the night enters your all.
What do you hear?
Yes!
Silence;
the sound of a whisper which
soothes a painful tear.

Ssh now.
Don't look.
Don't catch even a glimpse,
but let your eyes see;
so that the silence echoes in your breath
and the radiance of the sight consumes your all.
What do you see?
Yes!
Beauty;
the vision of a face which
heals a broken fear.

Ssh now.
Don't move.
Don't stir even a muscle,
but let your body sense
so that the beauty caresses your breath
and the tenderness of the moment removes your all.
>What do you feel?
>Yes!
>>Peace;
>>the presence of the one who
>>touches both far and near.

'Come to me, all you that are weary and are carrying heavy burdens, and I will give you rest. Take my yoke upon you, and learn from me; for I am gentle and humble in heart, and you will find rest for your souls.'

Matthew 11.29

Almighty God, in this quiet hour I seek communion with thee. From the fret and fever of the day's business, from the world's discordant noises, from the praise and blame of men and women, from the confused thoughts and vain imaginations of my own heart, I would now turn aside and seek the quietness of they presence. All day long have I toiled and striven; but now in the stillness of heart and the clear light of thine eternity, I would ponder the pattern my life is weaving.

John Baillie

Many people today look for silence, solitude and peace. They dream of places where they can rest, away from the daily hassles of living which tear them apart, exhaust them and leave them dissatisfied, wounded and bleeding – and always alone. But they won't necessarily find peace and quiet waiting for them in other places. There is a place within us where quiet reigns – the centre, our heart of hearts. There we can him who us the plenitude of silence. But who will guide us there? We must learn the way.

Michel Quoist

God is a being, still and peaceful, dwelling in the still eternity. Therefore should your mind be as a still, clear, mountain tarn, reflecting the glory of God as in a mirror, where the image is unbroken and perfect. Avoid, therefore, all that would needlessly disturb or confuse or stir up your natural mind, from without or from within. Nothing in the whole world is worth being disturbed about. Even the sins you have committed should humble you, but not disturb you. God is in his holy temple. Let all that is in you keep silence before him – silence of the mouth, silence of all desires and all thoughts, silence of labour and toil.

Gerhard Tersteegen

All I can prescribe out of my own experience is to abide patiently till the soul relaxes – it is sprung up. It needs to be let free from all thought and strain, and simply to bathe itself in the ocean of God's love. Do nothing itself – but let God do it all. Utter surrender. Then it becomes still, tranquil, and goes out to God and rests.

William of Glasshampton

Give peace, that is, continue and preserve it; give peace, that is, give us hearts worthy of it, and thankful for it. In our time, that is, all our time: for there is more besides a fair morning required to make a fair day.

Thomas Fuller

Give me, O God, a heart of joy
that rests in your peace
and a soul of tranquillity that delights in your beauty;
a spirit of glory that sings your praise,
a life of serenity at home in your presence
and a mind of quietness renewed by your Spirit;
through Jesus Christ our Lord.

Evelyn Underhill

My spiritual director is a hermit living in a tiny mountain shack. He rises at 1.30 a.m. to live his days and nights in the presence of God. I asked him straight out: 'How do you know when you are in the presence of God?' His answer says it all: 'When I experience *peace.*' *Tranquillity* expresses well this inner peace; it is a spiritual state characterized by freedom from fears and anxieties, from that which is disquieting or perturbing. Having all that truly matters, our so-called needs are pared to necessities – for sufficient is our daily bread alone.

W. Paul Jones

We loquacious human beings once again have an inner need of silence. If it were only absolutely still for a moment; if everything accidental, fortuitous and complex were silent; if the sound made by our senses ceased; then perhaps we could appreciate reality to the full, and love it with an undivided heart.

For anyone who wishes to hear what is true and real, every voice must for once be still. Silence, however, is not merely the absence of speech. It is not something negative; it is 'something' in itself. It is a depth, a fullness, a peaceful flow of hidden life. Everything true and great grows in silence. Without silence we fall short of reality and cannot plumb the depths of being.

Ladislaus Boros

Like a pillow to a tired head, be thou our God to us this night. Wearied with the conflict of life, worn by the burden of the day, we seek thee as our resting-place. May thy eternal calm descend upon our troubled spirits and give us all thy peace. Amen.

Anonymous

A peacemaker's quadrilateral

Kenneth G. Greet

My mother prayed that the First World War would be over before I was born. The Armistice was signed on 11 November 1918 and I arrived six days later. Perhaps this is why early on I put the search for peace at the top of my life's agenda.

This early resolve has been strengthened by subsequent events. When I was a teenager my best friend was a fine Christian lad called Max. We walked and talked together; it was a most enriching friendship. When the war came Max joined the merchant navy. His ship was torpedoed in mid-Atlantic and he was last seen swimming away in a sea of flame. My Bristol office was destroyed by enemy bombs one terrible night. When on another occasion I arrived home at 6 a.m. after a night of fire-watching at a local hospital, I found our neighbour's house destroyed and he lay dead in the rubble.

In these and a thousand other ways I found myself confronting the cruel and monstrous stupidity of war. At a crowded meeting in my native city the British Foreign Secretary declared, 'For every bomb the Germans drop on us we will drop two on them.' Two thousand people rose to their feet in frenzied applause. I think that I was the only one to remain seated. When a large part of Coventry was destroyed by enemy bombing it gave me no satisfaction to learn that Dresden had been reduced to rubble with the inevitable slaughter of thousands of German men, women and children.

As the years have passed the need for peace has grown increasingly urgent. The twentieth century was the most violent the world has known: millions died in war and the brightest brains were devoted to the production of increasingly destructive weapons. Whereas in the past black-coated preachers talked about the end of the world, now it is white-coated scientists who warn us that we possess the means of global annihilation.

What should be the Christian response to this dire situation? How can we become effectively involved in the search for a peace that is elusive but essential if humanity is to survive? I give my answer under four headings: a peacemaker's quadrilateral.

1. Thinking

Charles Wesley wrote:

> Jesus, confirm my heart's desire
>   To work, and speak and *think* for thee.

All three are important, but the primary task is to change the way people think, and that will mean doing some hard thinking ourselves.

In fact, the thinking of the Church about peace and war has undergone significant changes over the years. For the first three and a half centuries of its life Christians were forbidden by their leaders to carry arms; it was deemed contrary to the teaching and example of Jesus that they should be involved in the horrible slaughter which is war. Then, when the emperor Constantine embraced Christianity in 312AD and made it the state religion of the Roman Empire, he granted favours to the Church. In return the Church undertook to help in the military defence of the realm. Thus began the long connection between the Church and war.

From the start the Christian leadership was never very happy with this arrangement and sought to define the conditions that must be met if a war were to be deemed 'just' and therefore worthy of Christian support. It was always a doctrine of limitation: for example, no attack on civilians, force used to be proportional to the ends sought, a reasonable chance of success, and the cause must be just.

In practice it has always been next to impossible to confine war within the boundaries thus laid down, and in every age some Christians have refused military service. Significantly the Christian leadership in Britain condemned the invasion of Iraq on the grounds that this was a war that could not be called 'just' in those traditional terms. I think that we must now ask whether *any* war fought with modern weapons could be 'just'. The Church has some hard thinking to do.

2. Praying

Many years ago I resolved to pray every day for peace. Some people will no doubt say, 'You have wasted your time; millions of prayers have been offered and in spite of this wars continue with ever increasing savagery. There are nearly 40 armed conflicts raging at the present time. Evidently God, if he exists, is either deaf or does not care.'

This critical comment deserves a serious response. The first thing to be said is that prayers for peace are not intended to change God's mind, though some of them may sound like it. He is the God of peace and peace is his will. Our prayers, therefore, are for ourselves and for all our fellow human beings. We are asking God to help us remove the causes of war, and, referring back to my first point, to change the way people think. In other words, prayers for peace require commitment to a programme.

One of the hopeful features of life today is the number of peace groups that meet to study the practicalities of peacemaking, such as methods of conflict resolution, and opposing the international arms trade that feeds so much of the conflict around the world. These small initiatives are important, and so is the work of the UN and other large agencies that seek to create the conditions of peace.

3. Living

For all of us who seek to live the Christian life two things are of fundamental importance: text and context. Jesus condemned those who cried, 'Lord, Lord' but failed to *do* the Father's will (Matthew 7.21). They got the text right, but did not relate it to the context – the business of daily living. So far as peace is concerned there is little point in praying for it, or quoting biblical texts about it, unless in our own lives we are peace-ful people, makers of peace, bringing the spirit of reconciliation into all our relationships.

There is an ecclesiastical dimension to this. The world is not likely to take us seriously if we preach unity from a divided Church. The ecumenical quest is urgent. One of the scandals of history is that religion has often been the source and supporter of violence. There is much work to be done in exploring the Christian resources for non-violent ways of settling disputes.

4. Dreaming

One of the greatest utterances of modern times was Martin Luther King's 'I have a dream' speech. There is something mean and stunted about men and women who are unable to dream great dreams.

Every great achievement began with a dream. One of the thrilling privileges of my later years was to be closely associated with the building of the new Southlands College –

now part of the University of Roehampton. That wonderful and thriving campus began with a dream.

'If we can dream it, we can do it' runs the slogan written over the Epcot Park in Florida. But beware of the arrogance that assumes too much. This can lead to bulging silos packed with destructive weaponry. The Christian dream is of Christ's kingdom, prefigured in heaven and built on the earth, a kingdom of justice, mercy and love. It is for this that Jesus bade us strive and pray.

'Blessed are the peacemakers, for they will be called children of God.'

Matthew 5.9

> Waste of Muscle, waste of Brain,
> Waste of Patience, waste of Pain,
> Waste of Manhood, waste of Health,
> Waste of Beauty, waste of Wealth,
> Waste of Blood, and waste of Tears,
> Waste of Youth's most precious years,
> Waste of ways the saints have trod,
> Waste of Glory, waste of God –
>   War!

G.A. Studdert-Kennedy

I have seen war. I have seen war on land and sea. I have seen blood running from the wounded. I have seen men coughing out their gassed lungs. I have seen the dead in the mud. I have seen cities destroyed. I have seen 200 limping, exhausted men come out of line – the survivors of a regiment of 1,000 that went forward 48 hours before. I have seen children starving. I have seen the agony of mothers and wives. I hate war.

Franklin D. Roosevelt

These hearts were woven of human joys and cares
Washed marvellously with sorrow, swift to mirth.
The years had given them kindness. Dawn was theirs,
And sunset, and the colours of the earth.
These had seen movement and heard music; known
Slumber and waking; loved; gone proudly friended;
Felt the quick stir of wonder; sat alone;
Touched flowers and furs and cheeks. All this is ended.
There are waters blown by changing winds to laughter
And lit by the rich skies, all day.
And after,
Frost with a gesture, stays the waves that dance
And wandering loveliness. He leaves a white
Unbroken glory, a gathered radiance,
A width, a shining peace, under the night.

Rupert Brooke

Prayer is likely to be undervalued by all but wise people because it is so silent and so secret. We are often deceived into thinking that noise is more important than silence. War sounds far more important than the noiseless growing of a crop of wheat, yet the silent wheat feeds millions, while war destroys them. Nobody but God knows how often prayers have changed the course of history.

Frank C. Laubach

The past is prophetic in that it asserts loudly that wars are poor chisels for carving our peaceful tomorrows. One day we must come to see that peace is not merely a distant goal that we seek, but a means by which we arrive at that goal. We must pursue peaceful ends through peaceful means. How much longer must we play at deadly war games before we heed the plaintive pleas of the unnumbered dead and maimed of past wars?

Martin Luther King

Where people are praying for peace the cause of peace is being strengthened by their very act of prayer, for they are themselves becoming immersed in the spirit of peace.

George Macleod

Peace can only be manifested in society when there is peace within the human heart. The cause of peace is sometimes pursued with aggressiveness. This is the case when peace is no more than a concept than an ideal. ... Work for peace must first of all be a work within ourselves.

Bede Griffiths OSB

My personal vocation is to be a pilgrim of peace ...
We, as Christians, are on the side of non-violence
and this is in no way an option for weakness and
passivity. Opting for non-violence means to
believe more strongly in the power of truth,
justice, and love than in the power of wars,
weapons, and hatred.

Dom Helder Camera

Anyone can love peace, but Jesus didn't say, 'Blessed are the
peace-lovers.' He says 'peacemakers'. He is referring to a life
vocation, not a hobby on the sidelines of life.

Jim Wallis

*I'm a non-violent soldier. In place of weapons of violence,
you have to use your mind, your heart, your sense of
humour, every faculty available to you because no one has
the right to take the life of another human being.*

Joan Baez

I am a child of peace, and am resolved to keep the peace
for ever and ever, with the whole world, inasmuch as I
have concluded it at last with my own self.

Johann Wolfgang von Goethe

Pursuing peace and eschewing compromise

Harriet Harris

Making peace is hard work and Christians don't always excel at it. The bitter conflicts carried out in God's name suggest that the world might be a better place if people gave up religion. At the moment I'm frequently asked why churches fight so much over sexuality when Christians are supposed to be loving towards each other, and when we could be fighting poverty instead.

An initial answer to these understandable questions is that religious disputes are often intractable because people's faith matters to them deeply, so indifference is not an option or a virtue. Moreover, religion affects people in every aspect of their lives: from what they eat and who they eat with, to how they earn and spend their money. It shapes the pattern they give to their day, week and year. It informs the way in which they develop relationships, raise their children, and care for their sick and their dead. So a huge amount is at stake when people disagree over religion; and since we are only human, we easily get defensive. It takes a lot of energy to address disagreements, but it is energy the Church needs to spend (and it may not detract from our mission in meeting the needs of the poor – I doubt we have facts and figures on this). It is right for the Church, like any other family that is hurt and divided, to pay attention to its problems and try to heal them.

A longer answer is that it isn't obvious how to make peace. Achieving peace is more complicated than getting people to stop fighting. We call Jesus the Prince of Peace and yet he caused unrest, he argued with religious leaders, he said he came not to bring peace but a sword because his teachings were ones that would set brother against brother, sister against sister and parent against child. He was himself killed violently, probably because others were afraid of the potential he had to create civil unrest. Put like this, he wasn't a successful peacemaker. But the reason he wasn't successful was because he didn't settle for the things we sometimes mistake for peace.

Often when we pray for peace really we are praying for the status quo. We are praying that hostility and conflict won't come and disrupt our lives; for example, that the Church won't be divided, or that people's lives and communities won't be torn apart by war or acts of terrorism. But peace is more than the absence of conflict, and making peace involves more than putting down our arms.

Arriving at true peace usually involves both letting down our own defences, and addressing wrongs and injustice done to us and to others. That is why peacemaking disrupts the status quo. Peace is something we are to *pursue* (Hebrews 12.14), even if others have declared a standstill.

On the day in 2003 that Gene Robinson was elected Bishop of New Hampshire, and was thereby set to become the first openly gay bishop in the Anglican Communion, the Anglican Cathedral in Birmingham, Alabama, put up a black flag. In this chilling gesture, the Dean of the Cathedral was saying that Gene Robinson's appointment spells death for the Church. He was closing the door, or, to change the metaphor, he was saying we have reached the end and will not walk with Christian brothers and sisters any further down this road.

But if we are to pursue peace, we can't decide to come to a halt or close the door. We have to keep going. One of the reasons why making peace is so arduous is that it won't let us give up even when we're sure we've had enough. Giving up the pursuit can be self-righteous if, in effect, you are telling others that they are a lost cause.

However, that doesn't mean you have to meet your opponents halfway. Peace doesn't mean compromise, because compromise often harbours injustice, and then you have to ask who is carrying the cost. For example, if a church compromises by ordaining gay people but pretending not to, then gay people carry that cost because they are shamed by the church's official teaching and they are being asked to live a lie. Compromise is often damaging, and this needs to be said even though it is divisive to say it.

Making peace does not mean living with attitudes that are damaging for the sake of our all seeming to rub along together. In one church in my city, gay men call themselves heterosexual males with a same-sex attraction problem. (Gay women are probably completely invisible.) The Evangelical Fellowship for Lesbian and Gay Christians operates a helpline for Christians who have internalized such an ethos and who feel suicidal because of their attempts not to be gay. A true peace is one that will not create such casualties.

So I am impressed by the words of Tennessee Williams, the playwright from the American South, who insisted that moral issues are black and white, and if you think they are grey that's because a bit of the black has rubbed off on your soul. It is important for the sake of people's lives not to compromise with the idea that gay people are really heterosexuals with a problem. And it is not to the glory of God to preach a gospel that drives people towards death.

But then how might the churches arrive at a place where they can heal both those who have been stigmatized and driven to despair, and those who are afraid and offended by homosexuality? An attitude of no compromise comes with a moral health-warning: that moral certainty can lead to self-righteousness. We might think we are unreservedly on the side of God, and fall into the same trap as the disciples James and John. They thought they were closer to Jesus than all his other disciples, and that Jesus would want *them* sitting at his right and left side (Mark 10.35-45). Moral certainty can also instil fear in our brothers and sisters and drive them away. We need to remind ourselves that love surpasses all things. Don't hear me wrong, love sees justice done and won't settle for practices that fail to dignify people, but love then goes the extra mile. And going the extra mile is a good metaphor for pursuing peace. It says we have not come to the end of the road. When you've walked the extra mile with somebody, the barriers between you come down.

Jean Vanier, who has spent his life creating and living in community with people who are physically and mentally disabled, has said that prophets of peace don't contribute to people's fear, but rather open people's hearts to understanding and compassion. Opening people's hearts is the key to true peace. Compromise falls short of the mark because it is a matter of meeting each other halfway. An opening of hearts involves meeting each other where you each are and walking the road together. This means engaging properly so that some kind of breakthrough is achieved. Compromise leaves everyone dissatisfied in some way, whereas true peace moves us to a new level which is deeply satisfying and renewing. The process is harder work than striking a compromise, because it requires a deeper level of attentiveness, and usually involves dismantling our own defences. So making peace is a disruptive business, uncomfortable and painful. It challenges the status quo and the fragile arrangements we have for rubbing along together. But all the shake-up is what enables true peace to break out.

As God's chosen ones, holy and beloved, clothe yourselves with compassion, kindness, humility, meekness, and patience. Bear with one another and, if anyone has a complaint against another, forgive each other; just as the Lord has forgiven you, so you also must forgive. Above all, clothe yourselves with love, which binds everything together in perfect harmony. And let the peace of Christ rule in your hearts, to which indeed you were called in the one body.

Colossians 3.12-15

Lord, we pray for the power to be gentle; the strength to be forgiving; the patience to be understanding; and the endurance to accept the consequences of holding to what we believe to be right.

May we put our trust in the power of good to overcome evil and the power of love to overcome hatred. We pray for the vision to see and the faith to believe in a world emancipated from violence, a new world where fear shall no longer lead men and women to commit injustice, nor selfishness make them bring suffering to others.

Help us to devote our whole life and thought and energy to the task of making peace, praying always for the inspiration and the power to fulfil the destiny for which we and all people were created.

Week of Prayer for World Peace 1978, adapted

If you want peace of mind, do not find fault with others. Learn rather to see your own faults. Learn to make the whole world your own; no one is a stranger, my child, the whole world is your own.

Sri Sarada Devi

Too often peace is misunderstood as absence of challenge, disagreement, or even confrontation. Too often, in the name of peace, we hesitate to bring up disturbing issues. We remain silent, sweeping the debris of years under the rug where it silently pollutes the spiritual atmosphere. But honest disagreement or loving confrontation are not the same as harping criticism.

God's peace ... can exist even in the midst of open, deep differences. This is the peace founded on that vision of Isaiah in which all the different animals dwell together on God's holy mountain, in God's shalom. They live in peace not because they are alike, which they definitely are not, but because they care as much about one another's uniqueness and integrity as they do about their own.

Flora Slosson Wuellner

A church that doesn't provoke any crises,
a gospel that doesn't unsettle,
a word of God that doesn't get under anyone's skin,
a word of God that doesn't touch the real sin
of the society in which it is being proclaimed,
what gospel is that?
Very nice, pious considerations
    that don't bother anyone,
that's the way many would like preaching to be.
Those preachers who avoid every thorny matter
    so as not to be harassed,
    so as not to have conflicts and difficulties,
do not light up the world they live in.
They don't have Peter's courage, who told that crowd
where the bloodstained hands still were
that had killed Christ:
    'You killed him!'
Even though the charge could cost him his life as well,
    he made it.
The gospel is courageous;
it's the good news
    of him who came to take away the world's sins.

Oscar Romero

We can all walk together in hope;
celebrating that we are loved in our
brokenness,
helping each other,
growing in trust,
living in thanksgiving,
learning to forgive,
opening up to others,
welcoming them,
and striving to bring peace and hope to
our world.

Jean Vanier

Jesus requires us to take initiative for reconciliation. 'Blessed are the peacemakers ...' It is not enough to be peacekeepers, which would mean to avoid harming others. We have to do what we can to effect peace, and that means to do things that make for peace. Observe Jesus' illustration. If you are offering something on the altar of the Temple and remember that someone has something against you, 'leave your gift there before the altar and go; first be reconciled to your brother or sister, and then come and offer your gift (Matthew 5.23-24). ... Why does Jesus demand the impossible? That we may realize that we cannot do this without God's help.

E. Glenn Hinson

Space for God's peace

Chris Polhill

Peace is disturbing.

I take the young people from our church to the Camas adventure centre on the island of Mull. It is like a pilgrimage to get there, as we travel from train to train to boat to bus, and then for the last mile and a half we walk down the track. There is no vehicular access. It would be hard to find a more remote and beautiful place. The sea, with its continual movement and changing colours, steep granite hills and bracken, and in-between, just 20 yards from the shore, a row of old quarry/fisher cottages which the Iona Community has converted into an adventure centre for young people.

Young people love the freedom of Camas, away from parents and the restrictions of city life. They design their own worship space, the dormitories are off limits to all the adults except in emergency, and they are messy or tidy as they choose (mostly messy). They join the community life of the staff and volunteers there. This means they share the chores, which as well as the usual washing up and laying the table, includes chopping logs for the fire, emptying and cleaning the toilets; some general cleaning of the communal space, and gardening. There is no electricity or mains drainage at Camas. Any heating comes from the log fire, light from candles or torches, water is piped from a hillside spring, and toilet waste is composted (for trees, not vegetables I hasten to add). They share in the attitudes of the staff who accept people as they are, and watch for the troubled ones. Noticing someone's misery and doing something about it avoids many a conflict. They also share in the fun. With no TV for entertainment in the evening, we amuse ourselves as we sit round the fire. Songs, jokes, long games of Mafia fading into general chat and sleepiness. Then there is the total silence of the night, apart from the waves and wind, or the occasional burst of high spirits. A quiet and a darkness unknown to those who live in towns and cities, no orange glow but stars and moon, no traffic or noise from TV or CD, just nature's peace.

During the day there are adventurous challenges that test everyone's own limits. Always careful that no one feels a failure, the staff make it clear to everyone that different people have different fears and abilities, and what seems easy to one is hard, if not impossible, to another. So when it comes to abseiling, for example, just to walk to the quarry face is challenge enough for some, just to stand on the edge with all the gear on enough for others, and that is as acceptable as going blithely over the edge and bouncing down the long cliff-face. All the other challenges are treated in the same way, whether it's kayaking, fishing or anything else. There are environmental challenges too; Camas is so close to the natural world that environmental issues are easy to relate to. Twice a day there are reflection sessions, a kind of pre-worship, as most visiting groups do not relate to worship and faith. It means that all who go to Camas get this space to think about life and what is going on for them, to hear of others through poetry, Bible or sharing. Space to listen for God, and through it all the quiet and the space, the vastness of the sea and the sheer stunning beauty.

But the peace and quiet is disturbing. By the middle of the week there is usually a problem of some kind: some trouble boils up, or a row splinters the group, or there is a prolonged need to talk. Behind the disturbance every time are the issues that are troubling this particular group of people: the troubles that have been buried under the noise and busyness of everyday life, the fears that have not been acknowledged, the wounds of the soul that have never been recognized. I take young people from a pleasant, middle-class church – 'the group from heaven' the staff once called them when they visited the week after a particularly difficult group from a deprived inner city. But 'group from heaven' or not, I am humbled and shocked by the struggles these young people live with. Parents separated, or about to separate but it has not been spoken of, and all the attendant issues that their children have to find their way through and live with; their worries about the health of someone close to them; the death they have never grieved; the huge fear of the future; the scares of some peer pressures; will they pass exams, will they be able to say no to drugs? All big life difficulties, some of them not articulated before, some never shared with adults before, most of them not addressed at church but there in the hearts and lives of these younger brothers and sisters in Christ. Which disturbs my peace.

I notice myself that this is something peace does, just as quiet prayer does. The very quiet allows the things we bury under noise and busyness to surface and claim our attention. It is the most common reason for avoiding prayer, because in that inner quiet before God the troubles of our soul cannot be hidden, and in some unconscious way we know that and do not want to face whatever it is just yet, or ever. And this is one of the extraordinary contradictions of being human, because when I do look at whatever needs to surface, the peace that God offers weaves its own thread into my spirit, offers that deeper rest and healing that at the least helps me live another day with a particular struggle, and at best shines light in the darkness. So you would think that we would all turn to this quiet prayer quickly and gladly, yet I know that I, and others, resist it regularly, even strenuously. St Paul, in another context, puts it well: 'For I do not do the good I want, but the evil I do not want is what I do' (Romans 7.19).

I'm not even convinced that we all really want peace, not all the time. Individually our lives are filled with activity and busyness, perhaps with little oases of peace on holiday, but many of those are activity based now. We even need a certain amount of stress to stay healthy. As a race we show little practical willingness to live peacefully with each other, taxes are spent on defence or war and research on more weapons, but not on peacemaking and research into what will work. When we resolve issues with one enemy, as after the Cold War for example, we soon find another, like the Arab world or terrorism. Perhaps we are too disturbed by peace.

Life is worth the search for peace though, inner or outer. When we walk back up the track after a week at Camas I see young people who have grown in confidence and who have been strengthened and renewed. I too am refreshed within by my time there, even if I could do with more sleep. That disturbing peace has allowed space for God's peace.

O Lord, you have searched me and known me. You know when I sit down and when I rise up; you discern my thoughts from far away. ... If I take the wings of the morning and settle at the farthest limits of the sea, even there your hand shall lead me, and your right hand shall hold me fast.

Psalm 139.1-2, 9-10

> Listen, to the gentle lapping of the waves,
>   It is the breath of God.
> Listen, to the roaring of the waves
>   It is the power of God.
> Listen, to the shifting sands
>   It is the whisper of the Lord.
>
> Listen, to the music and the song
>   They are the joy of God.
> Listen, to the rain and the mist
>   They are the tears of God.
> Listen, to the sound of the snow
>   It is the sympathy of the Lord.
>
> Listen, to the restlessness of your heart,
>   the depth of your feelings,
>   the ideas of your mind,
>   It is the Lord who speaks.
> Listen, to the silence,
>   to the noise,
>   It is the Lord who speaks.

Anne Doyle

O Lord, my heart is all a prayer,
    But it is silent unto thee;
I am too tired to look for words,
    I rest upon thy sympathy
To understand when I am dumb;
    And well I know thou hearest me.

I know thou hearest me because
    A quiet peace comes down to me,
And fills the places where before
    Weak thoughts were wandering wearily;
And deep within me it is calm,
    Though waves are tossing outwardly.

Amy Carmichael

In quiet times of reflection, meditation and contemplation we can sometimes experience 'the peace of God which passes all understanding' at first hand. The peace of God may be experienced in many ways. For some this may be a certain oneness with the presence of the Father, the Son and the Holy Spirit. Others may experience this peace as a oneness with the presence of divine attributes such as light, life, joy, truth, love, grace, glory, power, goodness and so on.

William Sykes

Lord, you are my island, in your bosom I rest,
You are the calm of the sea, in that peace I lie,
You are the deep waves of the ocean, in their
    depths I stay,
You are the smooth white strand of the shore, in
    its swell I sing,
You are the ocean of life that laps my being,
In you is my eternal joy.

    Attributed to St Columba

God speaks not just on ink and paper but through every moment that we live and move and breathe. ... God sometimes speaks to us through events that disturb our peace. God acts through situations that so insistently intrude upon our lives that we cannot ignore them. Obedience to God is carefully listening and responding to the moments that prod us, spur us to action, and otherwise disturb our carefully constructed status quo.

    Thomas R. Hawkins

No peace lies in the future which is not hidden in the present instant. Take peace. The gloom of the world is but a shadow; behind it, yet within reach, is joy. Take joy.

    Fra Giovanni

Father God, your love surrounds us,
Cove and headland, sea and sand
Sing the praises of your beauty,
Show the hallmark of your hand.
Give us eyes to see your glory,
Ear attentive, hearts aflame,
Voices raised in nature's anthem
To the worship of your name.

God in Christ, your grace surrounds us,
Balm in sadness, hope in pain,
Costly love that seeks and finds us,
Bears us gently home again.
Grant to us, your pilgrim people,
Joy to serve and strength to lead,
Grace to share and live your message,
Gospel word and gospel deed.

Spirit God, your power surrounds us,
Power of tempest, wind and wave,
Source of sainthood, artist's vision,
Life that conquers sin and grave.
Pour your sevenfold gifts upon us
Minds to open, hearts to move.
Gather in the whole creation
To the banquet of your love.

Perran Gay

Hope in a violent world:
The Alexandria Peace Process

Andrew White

The relationship between religion and violence, both as a cause and a cure, as a means of bringing about reconciliation, is probably the most important issue facing the world today. Despite its importance, it is a topic that is often avoided at inter-faith consultations, for fear of causing offence.

Today, in a world post the attack on the Twin Towers, we do not have the luxury of avoiding the real issue. During the first Gulf War, President George Bush Snr stated that we were at a defining moment in history. We were not; it was an important moment. The events of 11 September 2001 were a defining moment in history. They were an attack on the heart of western democracy and power, pictures of which were seen in homes around the world. They were a defining moment because from this point on the foreign policy of the world's only superpower changed forever. Since this tragedy, the world has had to wake up to the fact that we live in the shadow of terrorism. We live in a world where there is an increasing divide between the West and the Islamic world.

The history of how Christianity, Islam and Judaism have related to each other is not good. Despite the nice stories that people are willing to recall, especially in the current climate, the record is deeply depressing. These days, much attention is given to the issue of Islamic terrorism, but the Church also has a history of violence. For example, there were infamous crusades of the Teutonic Knights against the pagan Baltic States, and the Protestant millenarian crusades of the Taborites in Bohemia. Then there was the Spanish Inquisition that, it could be argued, was a form of state-sponsored terrorism, and the 2,000 years of anti-Semitism that created the atmosphere in which the Holocaust could take place in the heart of Christian Europe.

In the present day, there are nearly always major religious elements in the conflicts that mar our world. In Europe, Africa and Asia, in the Balkans, Nigeria, the Ivory Coast, the Sudan, Pakistan and Indonesia there have been conflicts that heighten the divide between Islam and Christianity. However, it is the Israeli-Palestinian conflict – with its faltering peace process and continuing spiral of violence, tragedy and death – that clearly demonstrates the significant role of religions in the creation of conflict.

Although the conflict is not essentially a religious one, religion is regularly used to justify the nationalist claims and allegations of both communities. There is, therefore, an understandable desire to keep religion out of the conflict. 'Since the dangers of nationalistic religion are considerable, many political analysts and theorists of "Conflict Resolution" see religion in general as a negative factor in society. So they favour keeping religious personalities out of any peacemaking process.'[1] But Israel and Palestine are not like western liberal societies: the cultures of both peoples are not conducive to a total separation of religion and state. They live in a land that the three monotheistic faiths call holy; but the holy name of God has been desecrated by killing and bloodshed. Ultimately, we must realize that conflict usually results from the abuse of power. Both religion and politics can use and abuse power and often, when both are mixed, both can be corrupted.

The Oslo peace process was a secular peace plan imposed by secular leaders.[2] Despite a few years of relative peace, the process was a failure. The reasons for its destabilization were multi-faceted and complicated. Was it the pressure from the Clinton plan to come to final status agreement too quickly, or the lack of support from the Arab world for Arafat to accept the Camp David offer? Was it Sharon's ill-fated visit to Haram Al Sharif, the Temple Mount, or the frustrations of the Palestinian community at the failure really to deal with issues that affected their daily lives? There was also the issue of the return of refugees, and the actions of the renegade Abayat clan in Beit Jallah. They occupied Christian homes and shot missiles over to the Jewish neighbourhood of Gilo. *All* of these issues undoubtedly destabilized the peace process. More fundamentally, the peace process failed because it did not take seriously the religious dimensions of the conflict.

The Alexandria Declaration and beyond

In the autumn of 2000, soon after the beginning of the Intifada Al Aqsa, the Israeli Ministry of Foreign Affairs asked whether I would be prepared to help develop a religious track of the peace process, in the hope of making a positive contribution. This was something many Israelis and Palestinians had already been trying to achieve. The then Deputy Foreign Minister of Israel, Rabbi Michael Melchior, was appointed as the lead person from the Israeli side. Such a project needed the backing of Chairman Arafat. He clearly thought that it was a constructive idea, especially if the Archbishop of Canterbury could be involved. Chairman Arafat appointed Sheik Tal El Sider, an Imam and Minister within the Palestinian Authority, as the leader of the Palestinian delegation. Rabbi Michael Melchior and Sheik Tal El Sider proved to be a unique combination as they were both spiritual and political leaders who bridged the political-religious divide.

For several weeks, secret nocturnal meetings (between 10 p.m. and 3 a.m. or 4 a.m.) grappled with some of the most complex religious and political issues. The aim was to come up with a statement that could be agreed by all parties. Plans were made for a high-level meeting, which the Archbishop of Canterbury agreed to chair. The Grand Imam of the Al Azhar – the leading Sunni Islamic authority in the world at the time – added Islamic credibility to the process.

An historic declaration was to be the focus of a summit planned for early in 2001. At the heart of the deliberations was the idea of stopping the religious legitimization of the violence in the Holy Land, to show a united front from Jewish, Islamic and Christian leaders, and call for a religiously sanctioned ceasefire.

The Archbishop of Canterbury and his team visited Israel on 20 January 2001. First, he met Yasser Arafat, Prime Minister Sharon and Shimon Peres. All the meetings were positive and there was much expectation. It was to be the first time in history that such a high-level meeting had taken place between Israeli and Palestinian religious and political leaders. In the delegation were Sheik Tal El Sider, the Palestinian Minister of State, and the most senior Imams from Palestine. Elyahu Bakshi-Doron (the Sephardi Chief Rabbi), the Israeli Deputy Foreign Minister and Rabbi Michael Melchior (the leader of Meimad) headed the Israeli delegation. The Patriarchs and heads of the churches joined them.

The meeting
The gathering in Alexandria did not start well. Instead of starting by signing the Declaration and then working on the implementation, the Palestinian delegation decided that it no longer agreed with the wording of the document that had been prepared. A process of revision began immediately. Some struggled with the amendment of the Declaration,[3] but truly remarkable things were happening. Outside the deliberations the Rabbis were gathered around the Grand Imam of Al Azhar, and the Sheiks around the Chief Rabbi. An incredibly warm historic relationship was developing between these traditional enemies.

Within half an hour of receiving the final approval from both Prime Minister Sharon and Chairman Arafat there was a press conference revealing this historic agreement to the world. The Arab and Israeli media covered the story extensively, but some of the western media, including the BBC, did not know that the meeting was about to take place.

The future of the process

Developments since Alexandria are even more important than the document itself. Nobody involved was naive enough to think the Alexandria Declaration would provide the solution to the crisis, and although the cycle of violence continues, the Alexandria process remains a significant channel of Israeli and Palestinian engagement.[4] The international community now takes it seriously: it now realizes that the religious dimension of the peace process is far more than just a concern for issues connected to holy sites and Jerusalem. It is about preventing the Prince of Death from eclipsing the Tree of Life.

Both Rabbi Michael Melchior and Sheik Tal El Sider have been criticized for the position they have taken; yet both have remained resolute in this process. In a recent meeting in London, they both came under opposition from the Arab media. Taking Rabbi Melchior's hand, Sheik Tal El responded to the criticism: 'Rabbi Melchior is my brother and I will hold his hand and walk this long and difficult road of reconciliation until we can build a better world for our people, where we will live together in Peace.'

Sheik Tal El is a former leader of Hamas and a sign of real hope. He was caught up in violence, imprisoned, expelled, and left for days in the winter snow in Lebanon. Now he believes that peace is the only way. Sheik Tal El is also a reason for a commitment to continue to work with those who as yet do not hold to the validity of the way of peace. Usually, they do not because they have only seen the pain and brokenness of their own community and have not been able to transcend it to know the pain of the other.

The Alexandria process still has a very long way to go before the initial Declaration is fully implemented. However, a model and precedent has been set for religions to show corporately that religion can be a force for good as well as evil. Religion has power, and it is how this power is used that will determine if it can be a positive force towards reconciliation and conflict transformation.

Religion also faces another major challenge in the way that renewal and reform movements in all the Abrahamic faiths no longer accept the authority of orthodox, traditional leaders, whether Chief Rabbis, Grand Imams or Archbishops. Therefore, it is also necessary to engage with those who may not appear orthodox within their own tradition. It is these groups who often support violent philosophies. It is imperative that serious research begins to address this particular issue.

The history is not good, the present is bleak but if we are prepared to be as radical in our quest for reconciliation as the extremists are in their quest for violence we can build a different future; one where the Abrahamic faiths will travel the long and difficult journey of reconciliation together, even if they do shout at each other along the way.

NOTES

1. Yehezkal Landau, an Israeli peace activist, who goes on to state that, 'in the case of Israel/Palestine, this doctrinaire stance risks forfeiting the positive contribution that religious peacemakers can make'.

2. The Israeli-Palestinian Declaration of Principles (Oslo Accords) was signed in September 1993. The process was started in Madrid in 1991 and was effectively ended at the Taba Conference of January 2001.

3. Copies of the final declaration are posted on various sites on the internet. For example, see:
    www.anglicannifcon.org/Alexand-Declaration.htm.

4. For example, during the siege of the Church of the Nativity in Bethlehem, the Alexandria delegates were able to support the different complex aspects of the negotiations; and a siege at the Mukarta in Hebron was ended within two hours, thanks to the intervention of Sheik Tal El who went to rectify the problem.

All this is from God, who reconciled us to himself through Christ, and has given us the ministry of reconciliation ... So we are ambassadors for Christ, since God is making his appeal through us; we entreat you on behalf of Christ, be reconciled to God. ... As we work together with him, we urge you also not to accept the grace of God in vain. For he says, 'At an acceptable time I have listened to you, and on a day of salvation I have helped you.'

2 Corinthians 5.18, 20; 6.1-2

I believe that behind the mist the sun waits.
I believe that beyond the dark night it is raining stars.
I believe in secret volcanoes and the world below.
I believe that this lost ship will reach port.
They will not rob me of hope, it shall not be broken ...
My voice is filled to overflowing
with the desire to sing, the desire to sing.
I believe in reason, and not in the force of arms;
I believe that peace will be sown throughout the earth.
I believe in our nobility, created in the image of God,
and with free will reaching for the skies.
They will not rob me of hope, it shall not be broken,
it shall not be broken.

World Council of Churches 1985

I am a man of peace. I believe in peace. But I do not want peace at any price. I do not want the peace that you find in stone; I do not want the peace that you find in the grave; but I do want the peace which you find embedded in the human breast, which is exposed to the arrows of the whole world, but which is protected from all harm by the power of Almighty God.

Mahatma Ghandi

We can never obtain peace in the world if we neglect the inner world and don't make peace with ourselves. World peace must develop out of inner peace.

The Dalai Lama

To you, Creator of nature and humanity, of truth and beauty, I pray:
Hear my voice, for it is the voice of the victims of all wars and violence among individuals and nations.
Hear my voice, when I beg you to instil into the hearts of all human beings the wisdom of peace, the strength of justice and the joy of fellowship.
Hear my voice, for I speak for the multitudes in every country and in every period of history who do not want war and are ready to walk the road of peace.

Pope John Paul II

O Lord, grant us to love thee:
grant that we may love those that love thee;
grant that we may do the deeds that win thy love.

Muhammad

The essence of peace is to merge two opposites. Therefore your notions should not scare you if you see another, who absolutely opposes you, and you presume that there is no chance for peace between you two. On the same token when you see two individuals who are exactly two opposites, never say it would be impossible for them to reconcile. On the contrary, and this is the perfection of peace to make it between two opposites.

Rabbi Nachman of Breslav

It matters not whether a person be Jew or Gentile, male or female, free person or slave – it is according to his deeds that the Holy Spirit rests upon an individual.

Seder Eliyyahu Rabba

God is not a God of war and fighting. Make war and fighting to cease, both that which is against him, and that which is against your neighbour. Be at peace with all people, consider with what character God saves you.

St John Chrysostom

For me, hope has to do with this world and necessitates a readiness on the part of all people of good will to get involved in the task of making it a more just and better place for others to live in. ... All theories of the left and right which promised the inevitability of progress, a deterministic understanding of the forward movement of history, and the perfectibility of humans [have proved] to be totally unable to deliver. If that, in fact, is true, then where is hope to be found?

For me, hope comes from the fact that one human being has the capacity to feel the pain and share the joy of another. That means we are not locked into ourselves. The fellow-feeling and the compassion that another person's plight can engender in me is proof that we are not intended to live utterly selfish and self-seeking lives. There is a capacity for forming links with others, and it's upon that realisation that all notions of community are to be built.

Leslie Griffiths

Rainbow valley

Cecily Taylor

I know a far valley of green peacefulness –
and carry its slow wisdom.
Unhurried the seasons tiptoe behind each other;
there folk have sown and garnered the centuries through –
ways change but the valley stays itself.

Come back in another hundred years
– it seems to say –
the same lane will wander through leafed shadows,
all things return like the swallows
finding the same barn.

I remember the rainbow that blessed the hills
to continue the promise of day and night,
spring and harvest;
and how the largest moon
looked at us over the mountain.

Tread softly with the new day
butterflies own the bright flowers
the humble bees work on.
Disturb nothing
only listen to curlews
and the persistent cuckoo;

there is gold in the pasture
and hill-corn springing fresh once more.

Hoarding indelible imprints
of rock and meadow
I have never completely left –
still one with the cottage
sheltered from the north wind.

Ripple on little stream
I will return like the swallows
to drink again from your valley's chalice
all the peace it holds.

Blessed by the LORD be his land, with the choice gifts of heaven above, and of the deep that lies beneath; with the choice fruits of the sun, and the rich yield of the months; with the finest produce of the ancient mountains, and the abundance of the everlasting hills; with the choice gifts of the earth and its fullness, and the favour of the one who dwells on Sinai.

Deuteronomy 33.13-16

Saturday 21st June: walked up the hill to Ryedale lake. Grasmere looked so beautiful that my heart was almost melted away. It was quite calm, only spotted with sparkles of light; the church visible. On our return all distant objects had faded away, all but the hills. The reflection of the light bright sky above Black Quarter was very solemn.

Tuesday, 13th April: I walked along the lake side. The air becoming still, the lake was a bright slate colour, the hills darkening. The bays shot into the low fading shores. Sheep resting. All things quiet.

Dorothy Wordsworth

The wood I walk in on this mild May day, with the young yellow-brown foliage of the oaks between me and the blue sky, the white star-flowers and the blue-eyed speedwell and the ground ivy at my feet ... These familiar flowers, these well-remembered bird-notes, this sky, with its fitful brightness, these furrowed and grassy fields, each with a sort of personality given to it by the capricious hedgerows – such things as these are the mother-tongue of our imagination, the language that is laden with all the subtle, inextricable associations the fleeting hours of our childhood left behind them. Our delight in the sunshine on the deep-bladed grass today might be no more than the faint perception of wearied souls, if it were not for the sunshine and the grass in the far-off years which still live in us, and transform our perception into love.

George Eliot

Magnificent weather. The morning seems bathed in happy peace, and a heavenly fragrance rises from mountain and shore ... To exist is to bless; life is happiness. In this sublime pause of things all dissonances have disappeared. It is as though creation were but one vast symphony, glorifying the God of goodness with an inexhaustible wealth of praise and harmony.

Henri Frederic Amiel

Most of us will never know what it is that makes us turn aside and see the great sight that leads us to God. A red admiral butterfly fluttering its wings gently in the summer sunshine; a duck disappearing into the grey, dappled filminess of a lake in the autumn sunshine; an icy, still, frozen hawthorn branch, dripping its morning dew; a cluster of primroses hidden in the moss of a spring bank; a daffodil pushing through the gap between two concrete slabs, are all tiny glimpses ... Everyone will have their own memories of moments of deep detachment from the ordinariness of life, when the reality of God's beauty and omnipresence burst in upon us.

Anthony Hulbert

So I watched the grain week by week ... And it shone nights, as if there was a light behind it, with a kind of soft shining like glow-worms on a marish night. I never knew, nor do I know now, why corn shines thus in the nights of July and August, keeping a moonlight of its own even when there is no moon. But it is a marvellous thing to see when the great hush of the full summer and deep night is upon the land, till even the aspen tree, that will be ever gossiping, durstna speak, but holds breath as if she waited for the coming of the Lord.

Mary Webb

Went to Bickleigh Vale – a deep, narrow combe, running down out of the moor, with steep wooded slopes on either side, and deep down at the bottom the river Plym winding its way. The ground was carpeted with Anemones and Blue-bells and here and there Primroses, and the tall, handsome plants of the Wood Spurge were very conspicuous with their red stalks and pale green flowers. ... We walked four miles through the woods to Plym Bridge at the far end of the Vale. A Water Ouzel skimmed across the river and in under the arch-way of the old, grey, stone bridge, every cranny of which was green with tiny ferns.

Edith Holden

She could feel the earth moving, a great majestic motion, the fields and farm, the woods and hills were sailing away through that limpid sky. She held her breath in wonder, she felt as if she floated up and up into that silvery dome above her. Then she saw her first star, a pin-point deep in that sea of space. She lost it and found it again. Then another came out, and another, from nowhere. She began to count. They were all around her, the green sky had become radiantly, darkly blue, the trees were black, the earth flew like a great bird. ... So she got her first glimpse of infinity.

Alison Uttley

A peaceable economy

Peter Selby

At the height of the Jubilee 2000 campaign for the relief of the unrepayable debt there emerged a powerful critique of the economic system by Susan George, entitled *The Debt Boomerang* (Pluto 1992). It described, with strong and clear evidence, the way in which a system that landed the poorest of the nations in a situation of virtual bankruptcy (actually only individuals can go bankrupt – a relief not open to poor countries) led to disastrous effects on the lives of people in the *creditor* countries too.

These 'boomerangs' play their part in some of the most serious problems we face. The environment boomerang is the effect that the international economic system leads to the cutting down of rainforests, and the drugs boomerang leads to poor countries earning hard currency by growing and selling drugs. There are other boomerangs too: taxpayers in wealthier countries see some of their resources going into bailed-out banks which have contracted loans which can't be repaid. Wages in poor countries are depressed, with the result that jobs are lost in countries with higher wages and are exported to countries which are prepared – have to be prepared – to keep wages down in order merely to survive; and the so-called 'economic migrants' are in fact the result of the same economic system which means that those with the ability to escape from the poverty of indebted countries travel thousands of miles in search of the better lives they can't have at home.

But the most serious of the 'boomerangs' to which Susan George referred in 1992 was the role of international debt in causing social conflict, civil war and then international conflicts too. What was true in 1992 is certainly 'in our face' today. What we know to have been part of our own history – the economic roots of international conflicts – seems to surprise us still when we encounter it in the emergent histories of the world's poorest nations. We know, for instance, that the imposition of crippling reparations on Germany after the First World War produced unemployment on a dreadful scale throughout the world, and the part that played in the rise of Nazism hardly needs telling. A population suffering the effects of unrepayable debt imposed on its country was fair game for scapegoating ideologies, and all too ready to play its part in other people's evil designs.

Why should it be different in sub-Saharan Africa? Why should the burden of poverty not produce in other nations what we know it produced on the continent of Europe? How could it surprise us to find genocide on the continent of Africa, and lesser inter-tribal conflicts making development impossible, or military dictatorships arising which can waste valuable resources on prestige military projects? Those projects do nothing to help the poor, but in a situation of conflict are the means of buying support for the powerful against their enemies.

And why should we be surprised that economic imbalance should play such a large part in the continuing conflict in the Middle East? If 2005 turns out to be a year when peace in that troubled part of the world draws a bit nearer, it is bound to involve doing something about the scale of economic inequality in Palestine-Israel, an inequality fuelled by the unequal aid programmes of the wealthy countries.

Nor should we be merely depressed by the 'war boomerang' of our economic injustice. It is also a story with a hope line to it. For the fact is that the recognition of the part economics play in international affairs did bring about a situation after the Second World War where aid and debt relief enabled at last, after centuries, a hopeful continent and a peaceful one. Why should we be surprised, therefore, at the potential for peace that resides in the economic possibility we now have to bring about through a greater degree of international justice?

Yet we do continue to be reluctant to learn these lessons. The search for peace is constantly interrupted by the sound of war, and the economic roots of conflict need attention with an urgency we still do not feel. At the root of that lack of urgency lies our own dependence on the very economic system that has produced this injustice. The boomerang is cast, after all, from the wealthiest nations at the poorest in the form of our dominance of world markets; the boomerang returns, having inflicted its injury, to wound those who first sent it on its way.

The wound, for such it is, is an ever greater vulnerability to violence from within and without; like the ever increasing array of burglar alarms in a street, the sources of injury get ever nearer, and the cost of protection ever higher.

The search for peace is therefore bound to be a search for a peaceful economy, one that seeks both justice and sustainability as the keys to peace: justice, in that the widening gap between rich and poor is a principal source of violence and unrest; sustainability, in that living off tomorrow's bounty today produces ever fiercer competition for resources that are being used up can only lead to violent confrontation: not for nothing has it been prophesied by many observers that the wars of the future will not be over territory but over water supplies and firewood.

The image of a peace economy is that of the prophet: 'The wolf shall live with the lamb': it is a powerful image because it portrays precisely the end of the *predatory* relationship, and with it the end of bloodshed and fear. The predatory economy is the game in which there are victors and victims – until the day comes when all are victims. The search for peace has therefore to go on in the economy, not in the realms of military strategy: our search is for the *shared* prosperity which, according to the Scriptures, is the only prosperity that can last.

The life of the kingdom is one in which the landless shall inherit the earth and it will be the peacemakers, not those who dominate by weapon or money, who will be known as God's children.

May that kingdom of peace come quickly.

He shall not judge by what his eyes see, or decide by what his ears hear; but with righteousness he shall judge the poor, and decide with equity for the meek of the earth ... The wolf shall live with the lamb, the leopard shall lie down with the kid, the calf and the lion and the fatling together, and a little child shall lead them. ... They will not hurt or destroy on all my holy mountain; for the earth will be full of the knowledge of the LORD as the waters cover the sea.

Isaiah 11.3-4, 6, 9

Forgive us, O Lord,
when we listen, but do not hear;
when we look but do not see;
and when we feel, but do not act,
and by your mercy and grace
draw us into the righteous deeds
of your kingdom of justice and peace;
through Christ our Lord. Amen.

Maria Hare

We know that peace is only possible when it is the fruit of justice. True peace is the result of the profound transformation affected by non-violence which is, indeed, the power of love.

Perez Esquivel

Say 'No' to peace
if what they mean by peace
is the quiet misery of hunger,
the frozen stillness of fear,
the silence of broken spirits,
the unborn hopes of the oppressed.

Tell them that peace
is the shouting of children at play,
the babble of tongues set free,
the thunder of dancing feet,
and a father's voice singing.

Say 'No' to peace
if what they mean by peace
is a rampart of gleaming missiles,
the arming of distant wars,
money at ease in its castle,
and grateful poor at the gate.

Tell them that peace
is the hauling down of flags,
the forging of guns into ploughs,
the giving of fields to the landless,
and hunger a fading dream.

Brian Wren

The pursuit of peace and progress cannot end in a few years in either victory or defeat. The pursuit of peace and progress, with its trials and its errors, its successes and its setbacks, can never be relaxed and never abandoned.

Dag Hammarskjold

Peace cannot be achieved through violence, it can only be attained through understanding.

Ralph Waldo Emerson

Grant to us, O Lord,
fullness of faith, firmness of hope and fervency of love.
For the sake of your gospel may we sit loosely to our wealth
and daily embrace you in the poor of the world.
As we rejoice in your generosity
so may we give ourselves in the service of others,
through Christ our Lord. Amen.

Thomas More

God's love for me precedes any achievement on my part. It is all of grace. This speaks volumes about my value and that of other human beings – our worth in the sight of God is intrinsic to who we are. It does not depend on any extraneous thing. Consequently *every* human being is of immense, of infinite value. This truth is subversive of all injustice, oppression and exploitation.

Desmond Tutu

A peacemaker is anyone who brings healing in this world.

Thomas Keating

We are called to be neighbours, and to be neighbours to other persons. Today I think the poor are the 'distant' ones for us. They are 'distant' in terms of our categories, our way of being human beings and even Christians. We need to enter into the world of the poor. It means to leave our way today and go to the distant one, our neighbour. And I think to try to leave our way and to make neighbours is one way to choose life. As Christians we must convert the distant person into a close person through our commitment. It is a way to give life and to choose life.

Gustavo Gutierrez

Saint Mark's missing verse

Philip J. Morse

Most of the time my life occupies the space of Saint Mark's missing verse. I quote it often. In most circuits in which I have served as a minister, I have taught Methodist local preachers on trial, and I always ask them to compose for me a bijou sermonette on Mark 15.48. They go away with enthusiasm, but return rapidly to inform me of my mistake – 'There are only 47 verses in Saint Mark's Gospel!' Oh no, there is no mistake. Mark 15.48 is where I am.

In scriptural terms, of course, they are correct, but metaphorically I have not met one yet who has not missed the point. Consider Mark 15.47: 'Mary Magdalene and Mary the mother of Joses saw where he was laid.' The *actual* last verse of Mark's fifteenth chapter describes the witnesses to the entombment of Christ – and what they witnessed. They saw Joseph of Arimathea enshroud the dead body of Jesus, lay him in a rock-cut tomb, and roll a great stone against the door of the tomb. They saw what he did and where he did it, and they saw that Jesus was dead. All this must have happened before sunset on the evening of Good Friday, because sunset would herald the beginning of the sabbath when ritually they could do nothing.

The next *actual* verse in Mark's Gospel is 16.1: 'When the sabbath was over ...'. The sabbath was over at sunset on the Saturday evening (did they buy the spices after that?), but as it would not have been practical to perform the appropriate rituals of the anointing of a corpse in the darkness of a tomb at night, they waited until the earliest practical opportunity, which was at sunrise on the first day of the week – Sunday, in our terms.

So, what did they all do between sunset on Good Friday and sunrise on Easter Day? What did they do on Saturday? If Mark had written just one more verse to his fifteenth chapter – 15.48 – he might have told us. But Mark 15.48 is Saint Mark's missing verse. And it is where I am, because, like the disciples of Jesus on that Saturday, I have seen death and the body (many bodies!) laid in the tomb, but I have not yet seen, with my own eyes, as the disciples did on Easter Day, the dawn of resurrection and the stone rolled back. I have as yet no personal experience of Job's assured future, either in respect to myself or to those whom I have loved: 'For I know that my Redeemer lives, and that at the last he will stand upon the earth; and after my skin has been thus destroyed, then in my flesh I shall see God ...' (Job 19.25-26), neither have I had the 'other' (Beloved?) disciple's opportunity: 'and he saw ...' (John 20.8).

I cannot claim that disciple's alleged disadvantage: 'For as yet they did not understand the Scripture, that he must rise from the dead' (John 20.9). Apart from the fact that that Scripture is neither specified nor clear – nor can it refer to a scriptural reference written *after* the event – the disciples may not have read and remembered a scriptural reference, but they had heard the truth from the Master's own lips, and that should have been even more compelling: 'Then he began to teach them that the Son of Man must ... be killed, and after three days rise again. He said all this quite openly' (Mark 8.31-32.)

So each present day is lived within the confines of a finite yet lifelong Saturday. I know what happened on Friday, but I have not personally witnessed what will happen on Sunday. I have only the promise of it, through the written record of the Master's own words and deeds. The original disciples only lived through one day between sunset on Good Friday and sunrise on Easter Day, but I live that day every day of my life, as do we all. It is the day that divides faith from knowledge, belief from sight, and it is the 'now' when the bereaved gather around an open grave before the coffin is lowered and when they know what Paul really meant when he spoke of 'the last enemy'.

I suppose that it has been the anguish and confusion on the faces of the faithful bereaved at the graveside, balanced between faith and sight, which have caused me to think so much about Saint Mark's missing verse. Until I understand the nature of the day – the Saturday – I can neither anticipate nor begin to experience the peace of the risen Christ of Easter Day.

Am I then only a prisoner in an endless, earthbound day, because 'with the Lord one day is like a thousand years, and a thousand years are like one day' (2 Peter 3.8)? I think that there is a way to see through to God's perspective of the Easter dawn from the mortal Saturday in which we live, and in so doing to anticipate the peace of the risen Christ before his appearing.

In the first place, there is a remarkable simplistic logic that we may apply. No matter how long Saturday appears to us to be, we know that unless God stops time, Sunday will come as the next day. Sunday's dawn will break. Shall we see Sunday's dawn before our Saturday's sun has set? Perhaps not, logically or otherwise: 'All of these died in faith without having received the promises, but from a distance they saw and greeted them ...' (Hebrews 11.13). Were those who died 'on the Saturday' denied what was promised them? No, for God 'has prepared a city for them' (Hebrews 11.16).

Secondly, it is the testimony of so many Christians living through this earthbound Saturday that the power of God's following resurrection day flows back into our preceding day. Although we ourselves have not yet personally walked with Cleopas and his friend on 'tomorrow's' Emmaus Road, so many of our experiences on our Christian pilgrimage cause our hearts to burn within us, suggesting that the risen Lord is already walking with us. Our experiences now are an anticipation of God's day of resurrection, a 'foretaste of the heavenly banquet', if you wish.

Thirdly, we fret and wrestle with what we are doing on our metaphorical mortal day between Good Friday and Easter Day, but what has the Church believed that Jesus was doing on that first Saturday between Good Friday and Easter Day? It was a speculative though logical deduction in faith, I suppose, but the Apostles' Creed stated our Christian belief clearly: 'He descended to the dead.' The line is a reference to the so-called 'harrowing of hell' when Christ visited those who had lived and died before his earthly incarnation, giving them the opportunity of release, and it draws its inspiration from a reference in 1 Peter: 'He was put to death in the flesh, but made alive in the spirit, in which also he went and made a proclamation to the spirits in prison, who in former times did not obey ...' (1 Peter 3.18-20). Andrea Mantegna and his contemporaries painted the imagined occasion several times, powerfully and movingly, under the title, 'Descent into Limbo'. Look at Adam's face in the 1492 canvas – a medieval myth, or a logical hope? But if Christ visited those prisoners, can he not also visit Saturday's prisoners?

In February 1997, after conducting my mother's funeral, as she had instructed me to do, I buried her ashes next to the casket containing those of my father. Romantically, stupidly perhaps, I made sure that the two caskets were touching, face to face. It felt like a Saturday, but I do not think that it was. It was, however, on the metaphorical Saturday in which I live – the Saturday of Saint Mark's missing verse.

'The day of resurrection, earth, tell it out abroad!' That day, for us, shall be God's tomorrow, and until it dawns, we shall watch and we shall pray, until the risen Christ himself comes even to us, shows us his wounds now glorified, and gives us in full his eternal peace.

Therefore, since we are surrounded by so great a cloud of witnesses, let us also lay aside every weight and the sin that clings so closely, and let us run with perseverance the race that is set before us, looking to Jesus the pioneer and perfecter of our faith, who for the sake of the joy that was set before him endured the cross, disregarding its shame, and has taken his seat at the right hand of the throne of God.

Hebrews 12.1-2

He is the lonely greatness of the world –
    (His eyes are dim),
His power it is holds up the cross
    That holds up him.

He takes the sorrow of the threefold hour –
    (His eyelids close),
Round him and round, the wind – his Spirit – where
    It listeth blows.

And so the wounded greatness of the World
    In silence lies –
And death is shattered by the light from out
    Those darkened eyes.

Madeleine Caron Rock

Today a grave holds him
who holds creation in the palm of his hand.
A stone covers him
who covers with glory the heavens.
Life is asleep and hell trembles
and Adam is freed from his chains.
Glory to your saving work
by which you have done all things!
You have given us eternal rest,
your holy resurrection from the dead.

From an Orthodox liturgy for Holy Saturday

Lead us into the silence that can both listen and hear;
into the openness that can receive, into the rest that holds us
in your way.
Lead us within the mystery of silence.
Help us to hear the great silence at the heart of God.
Help us to trust the eternal listener in silence, the mysterious
presence at the heart of silence that sustains, listens within
and to the depths that we shall never exhaust or fathom.

Anonymous

May the Light of lights come
   To my dark heart from thy place;
May the Spirit's wisdom come
   To my heart's tablet from my Saviour.

Be the peace of the Spirit mine this night,
Be the peace of the Son mine this night,
Be the peace of the Father mine this night,
Each morning and evening of my life.

Carmina Gadelica

In the Bible the word *peace, shalom,* never simply means the absence of trouble. Peace means everything which makes for our highest good. The peace which the world offers us is the peace of escape, the peace which comes from the avoidance of trouble, the peace which comes from refusing to face things. The peace which Jesus offers us is the peace of conquest. It is the peace which no experience in life can ever take from us. It is the peace which no sorrow, no danger, no suffering can make less. It is the peace which is independent of outward circumstances.

William Barclay

I know that right is right: that givers shall increase,
That duty lights the way for the beautiful feet of peace;
That courage is better than fear, and faith is truer than doubt;
And fierce though the fiends may fight, and long though the Angels hide,
I know that Truth and Right have the Universe on their side;
And that somewhere beyond the stars is a Love that is stronger than hate;
When the night unlocks her bars, I shall see him – and I will wait.

Anonymous

CHRIST: I'm going out into the light, for this is the dawn of Easter. Joseph's garden is bright with dew beneath my feet. The eastern sky is tinged with blood. What currency blood is! It alone buys. I'm buying everyone. I'm buying sorrow and pain, blasphemy and perdition. On Calvary hill I spat out the sponge dipped in vinegar, but now I'm swallowing Death so that it won't go on sprouting. It will be the final horror of my passion. And then music, music until the end of the world.

Luigi Santucci

Inner and outer peace

Sheila O'Hara

Christmas is over. It is time to welcome the new year of 2005, when many of us pray and preach about the gospel of peace. In his youth the Irish poet W.B. Yeats had already learned that 'peace comes dropping slow'. Reflecting on this experience in his old age, he made a harsher comment. The 'masterful images' that dominated his earlier years urged him to look outwards and upwards, ignoring the vast uncharted territory of his own heart. Yeats believed that the stable centre of his heart had crumbled. Over the years it had been starved of nurture. The ladder of external 'masterful images', which he had been climbing since the days of his youth, was not grounded in his neglected inner world.

The truth is that our journeys inwards and outwards need to be made simultaneously. Shakespeare speaks of the vast world known to the Elizabethans as the macrocosm, the external universe that awakens our fear, our wonder and our creative instincts. At the same time he explores the 'little world of man', that hidden microcosm, an equally vast area of inner consciousness. In *King Lear* the outer storm on the heath replicates the inner storm of the king's personal life.

We tend to speak of Jesus' public life to the exclusion of his equally vibrant inner life, where in prayer he explored his own identity. It is here that he experienced being one with his Father. Moving through prayer into the mystery of this 'oneness', he encountered the reality that informed and sustained his public mission. These prolonged periods of prayer tended to occur either before or after critical public occasions. The revelation at his baptism in the Jordan, where he is publicly acknowledged as the 'Beloved Son', at one with his Father and the Holy Spirit, precedes the 40 days of prayer and temptation in the desert. St Luke (4.14-19) recounts that he returns from the desert to Nazareth where he publicly identifies himself with the Isaiah passage, 'He sent me to bring the good news to the poor.' So begins his public ministry. Similarly, his hours of agonizing prayer in Gethsemane bear fruit in his words from the cross: 'Father, forgive' (Luke 23.34). At the Last Supper Jesus warns that his peace is not one the world can give (John 14.27). After his resurrection he speaks and acts as the peace-bringer, ' "Peace be with you." After he said this, he showed them his hands and his side' (John 20.20). It would seem that the creation of peace and the acceptance of suffering go hand in hand!

It has been said that peacelovers are two a penny and peacemakers rare birds! In our desire to create peace we often fall into the trap of imagining that our efforts will offer solutions to the problem. Yet the injustices that so often destroy the hope of peace arouse in peacelovers angry reactions that rarely foster a climate of peace. Does George W.

Bush's decision to conquer one form of terror with a more fearful one ensure a lasting peace?

The personal inward and outward journeys do not provide facile solutions to the strife in our world, but they do foster in us a sense of balance as we come to understand human dignity both in relation to ourselves, to others, and to the universe. As Christians we accept that God is in us and around us, in human affairs and in all of his creation. This belief does not in itself create peace, but it does permit us to enter into a deeper understanding of life, a perspective other than the norm. Our faith is a mystery, a 'mysterium fidei'. One can argue that even Jesus himself was a disturber of the peace, upsetting the imperial Pax Romana! Nevertheless it is clear that he honoured the dignity of each person with whom he came in contact. He accepted all those whom he encountered, as they were, irrespective of their beliefs and cultural differences, honouring, as Rabbi Jonathan Sacks would say, 'the dignity of difference'.

We cannot begin to create genuine communities, even within the ambience of our own Christian denominations, unless we accept the dignity of difference – surely a fundamental principle in establishing the peace of which Jesus speaks. We come to honour our own personal identity more fully as we travel in prayer along our inner journeys, discovering the mystery of our beings as children of God. It is with this understanding of ourselves that we learn to accept the sacredness of others, of all others, irrespective of their faith or philosophical stances, or their cultures.

In a recent pamphlet, entitled *Presence*, by a Benedictine monk, Thomas Cullinan, published by CAFOD, he writes:

> Jesus' presence, his preaching, and the way he relates to people and calls them forth, heightens the dignity of the human person. It means that people are far more important than human society ... Jesus is generating the real possibility that people can live in different ways, and honour each other, can discover relationships, structures and ways in which as society we can honour the potential divinity of people ... The creative imagination of the prophet is generating the real possibility, not just as an ideal, that people live in new ways in practice. That is why it was and is so threatening.

The passage envisages a starting point for society radically different from those that now operate in our world. If we began by accepting the unique integrity of each human being, as Jesus did, we could arrive at a new way of living in society, even in the global context. The prevailing structural organizations of peoples and cultures have not noticeably fostered a climate of peace among us. Sometimes it may be wiser to retrace our journeys in order to find a new path into the future. In itself that is quite a challenge. No wonder, then, that Thomas Cullinan above speaks of the new way as threatening. He also refers to the imagination of the prophet. To retrace our steps, to begin again, to set out on an uncharted course, demands from us a prophetic approach, a prophetic vision. Isaiah's dialogue with God (Isaiah 6) is a classic example of the journey inwards that sent the prophet outwards: 'Then I heard the voice of the Lord saying, "Whom shall I send, and who will go for us?" Who will be my messenger? And I said, "Here am I; send me!" ' (Isaiah 6.8).

The cynic will reject all this. How can we begin again? How is it possible to move beyond our sinfulness and inclination to evil? Well! Jesus spoke of his peace as being unique, quite distinct from the peace being offered by the world. His peace overrides cold reasoning and blind impulse. Its starting point is the love of all creation.

The journey from the personal to the global scene is a difficult one, yet we speak today of a growing one-world consciousness among us. Globalization, with all its ambiguities, challenges us to seize the opportunity of recognizing unity in this marvellous diversity, so loved by God. Let us not lose hope because of our seeming helplessness. The magnitude of the challenge could depress us. Who would not feel discouraged by the enormity of the world's troubles? But there are small signs of hope. The 'Drop the Debt' campaign brought some immediate relief to the poorest countries in our world. In our thousands, with so many from other faiths and none, we came into the market-place to challenge the rich governments of the world, and they heard us! We walked peacefully into the arena where sadly our presence and our influence is so often significantly absent. The antagonism of powerful interests will confront us, but in God's name we will persevere. Vox populi in this context is surely Vox Dei.

Archbishop Oscar Romero, who was murdered at the altar as he was celebrating Mass, used to counsel his flock to remember that no great plan would be completed in the life of one generation.

'This is what we are about,' he said.
'We plant the seeds that one day will grow.
We water the seeds already planted,
knowing that they hold future promise.
We lay foundations that will need further development.
We are workers, not master builders, ministers, not messiahs.
We are prophets of a future that is not our own.'

In the morning, while it was still very dark, he got up and went out to a deserted place, and there he prayed.

'I have said this to you, so that in me you may have peace. In the world you face persecution. But take courage; I have conquered the world!'

Mark 1.35; John 16.33

Risen Jesus,
we thank you for your greeting,
'Peace be with you.'
The shalom of God, deep lasting peace;
peace that brings inner calm;
that keeps a person steady in the storm;
that faces the persecutor without fear
and proclaims the good news with courage and with joy.

This is the peace that reconciles
sister to brother, black to white,
rich and poor, young and old;
but not a peace that is quiet
in the face of oppression and injustice.
This is peace with God,
the peace that passes understanding.

John Johansen-Berg

Jesus often withdrew to seek solitude. While others were lulled to the rest of sleep, Jesus was drawn to the rest of gaining strength and direction for his next phase of mission. ... His spirit was always rested, his private world ordered. Without this kind of rest our private world will always be strained and disordered.

Gordon MacDonald

We need to be taught how to live, how to use time aright, for it is [God's] gift. God alone can teach us how to order our days; he alone can bring peace and order into our lives. Here no discipline is more important than the regular practice of prayer, which involves a deliberate choice of time for thought and prayer, for 'worship is the keystone of order, and therefore of peace, which is the tranquillity of order'.

Olive Wyon

When peace dwells in a person's heart it enables them to contemplate the grace of the Holy Spirit from within. The person who lives in peace collects spiritual gifts as it were with a scoop, and sheds the light of knowledge on others. All our thoughts, all our desires, all our efforts, and all our actions should make us say constantly with the Church, 'O Lord, give us peace!' When a person lives in peace, God reveals mysteries to them.

Seraphim of Zarov

The fruit of silence is prayer.
The fruit of prayer is faith.
The fruit of faith is love.
The fruit of love is service.
The fruit of service is peace.

Mother Teresa

Honour peace more than anything else. But strive first of all to be at peace in yourself.

John of Apamea

Once, when I was particularly depressed, a friend and pacifist from Holland told me something very beautiful: 'The people who worked to build the cathedrals in the Middle Ages never saw them completed. It took two hundred years and more to build them. Some stonecutter somewhere sculpted a beautiful rose; it was his life's work, and it was all he ever saw. But he never entered into the completed cathedral. But one day, the cathedral was really there. You must imagine peace the same way.'

Dorothee Soelle

It isn't enough to talk about peace. One must believe in it. And it isn't enough to believe in it. One must work at it.

Eleanor Roosevelt

As I see it, to live a day at a time means to accept the happiness which each day brings without spoiling it by deploring that I may not be able to enjoy the pleasures which I supposed the years had in store for me. It means to do that bit of my task which is within my power today without worrying about whether I shall be able to finish it, and leaving it in God's hands to make what use of it he can. It means bearing the day's suffering, if suffering there is to be, in the strength that the day brings, without wondering how I shall endure the more severe trials that may come, but believing that 'as thy days, so shall thy strength be'.

Leslie J. Tizard

Knowing that we are fulfilling God's purpose is the only thing that really gives rest to the restless human heart.

Charles Colson

The search for peace

John Morrow

There is a problem with the word 'peace'. It can be used in so many different ways and with differing meanings. In popular usage it simply means an end to or an absence of violence. This is a rather negative definition although not to be despised, especially in situations where there has been a long period of conflict. A ceasefire can be a very important first step. However, unless the process continues in more positive ways it remains very unstable.

A very traditional method of creating a form of peace is by scapegoating. If a majority of people come to agree that the source of their troubles is a particular group or individual they can unite together to expel or defeat them. Most major wars have at least a degree of scapegoating. However, it is a self-deceptive mechanism because it allows us to project all our fears and the blame for our difficulties outside ourselves! Sooner or later the unity or peace built by scapegoating breaks down when the harsh fact that we are not all innocent reasserts itself and new scapegoats have to be found. In Ireland it is so easy for us to blame the terrorists for our troubles, or the politicians, or the Roman Catholic Church, or British Imperialism etc. etc. But it is only when we begin to accept some share of responsibility for our conflicts that we can begin to build real peace.

The Hebrew word Shalom is translated as Peace in English. But it is a very rich and positive word in its meaning. It refers to social and personal wholeness. It means right relationships, justice and truth. For Christians this is most fully embodied in the life, death and resurrection of Jesus Christ. In much of his teaching Jesus warned against 'false peace'. He even said that the search for true peace would at times involve division when we find we have to challenge those things which do not 'make for peace'. A lot of his ministry was about healing, wholeness and the restoration of broken relationships. In Ireland we have a long history of conflict resulting in a legacy of deep wounds, both mental and physical, prejudice and distrust. Probably the most difficult task is to learn to acknowledge our need for healing.

A major part of peacemaking is how to deal with our past. How do we find a way of moving beyond it without simply repressing it? There are so many aspects of this including forgiveness, repentance, truth and justice, if we are to achieve real reconciliation. Can we find ways of living with our differences? One of the most illuminating passages in the New Testament, giving us a model for 'community life', is found in 1 Corinthians 12.12-31, where Paul develops the image of 'the body'. It is a picture of 'Unity in Diversity' where every part has a unique function but each part is dependent on all the others. It is a model of diversity and interdependence. Community is not based on uniformity. When we try to make everyone the same we destroy community. But differences can be a cause of rivalry unless we realize that they are potentially a source of enrichment.

Some differences are not easily compatible because we fear that we might be swallowed up by our rivals. Learning how to live with differences of culture, race and nationality is not easy. There are not many models in the world. Usually majorities are the winners and others are the losers! So at the heart of peacemaking is the creation of trust. When we live our lives separately and rarely meet, fear is easily nurtured and trust is difficult to create. Trust-building begins by taking small steps. It involves taking a risk so as to open up the possibility of a new relationship and better understanding.

Throughout my involvement with the Corrymeela Community I have witnessed many examples of those small steps. A bereaved mother, whose son was murdered by paramilitaries, reached out to meet other bereaved people and they learnt how to support each other in their loss. Couples who married across the cultural and religious divide set up an association to share their experiences. They have often influenced the churches to develop joint pastoral care. Parents who wanted their children to be educated together pioneered the establishment of integrated schools. There are now almost 50 such schools and it all started with 12 children in a disused scout hut. Even ex-prisoners' families have come together to seek mutual understanding. In all of these groups the process of trust, forgiveness, co-operation and understanding develops slowly but surely. But nothing happens unless someone takes a risk – a small step. People are at very different stages so what might be a trivial thing for one person might be very significant for another.

In the midst of all this there are constant discouragements. Those who are afraid of change or have vested interests in the status quo will seek to put obstacles in our way. It requires a lot of courage to stand up and be counted, as we have seen recently when a family publicly challenged a paramilitary group to acknowledge collusion in the killing of their brother. But there are countless examples of such courage unknown to us all, going on every day. The willingness to speak truth to power, whether that power be government agencies or paramilitary groups, is a powerful witness for peace. It is a special challenge to the churches who are tempted to opt out or hide their heads in the sand. Peacemaking is a way of life. Above all it involves the transformation of ourselves if we are to be agents of the transformation of society. Without God's help we soon give up but with his help all things are possible. When the unexpected happens it shows the Spirit at work in the world.

For just as the body is one and has many members, and all the members of the body, though many, are one body, so it is with Christ. For in the one Spirit we were all baptized into one body – Jews or Greeks, slaves or free – and we were all made to drink of one Spirit.

1 Corinthians 12.12-13

We frail humans are at one time capable of the greatest good and, at the same time, capable of the greatest evil. Change will only come about when each of us takes up the daily struggle ourselves to be more forgiving, compassionate, loving, and above all joyful in the knowledge that, by some miracle of grace, we can change as those around us can change too.

Maíread Maguire

There is no way to peace. Peace is the way.

A.J. Muste

Serving peace is not easy. Often it is harder to seek dialogue with someone close at hand – a spouse, relative, co-worker, employer, or neighbour – than with a distant enemy seen only on television screens.

Jim Forest

In the heat of memory we recall
that for every victory
there is a loss;
that for every ceasefire,
there is a sniper;
that for every liberation,
there is a prison;
that for every peace agreement,
there is continued conflict,
if not above our skies,
if not in our waters,
if not in these islands,
if not on our doorstep,
then in some forgotten field.
We will remember them ...

Janet Lees

I believe that only in broken gleams has the Sun of Truth yet shone upon human beings. I believe that love will finally establish the kingdom of God on earth, and the cornerstones of that kingdom will be liberty, truth, brotherhood and service.

Helen Keller

The earth is too small a star and we too brief a visitor upon it for anything to matter more than the struggle for peace.

Colman McCarthy

I, like all of us, am a creature of my environment. For too long I lived in our divided society and my eyes were blinkered. Sometimes I saw and did not realise. Other times I did not see, and because I did not see, I did not realise. Today it is different. I have seen, and now I know ... what our divisions have done to us. And because I have seen and realised, I dare not stand idly by. The call is clear and I must try to make an answer, however imperfect or hesitating that answer may be.

Eric Gallagher

Risen, reigning Christ,
in you past, present and future
are brought together in one great hope.
Renew our faith in you,
so that the past may not hinder us,
nor the present overwhelm us,
or the future frighten us.
You have brought us this far,
continue to lead us
until our hope is fulfilled
and we join with all God's people
in never-ending praise;
for your name's sake. Amen.

Prayer from CTBI material for
the Queen's Golden Jubilee 2002

[In the New Testament] there is the revelation of God's saving love for us and the new commandment that we are to love others as Christ loves them (cf. John 13.34). Here we come to the heart of the new covenant and to the Gospel of peace. We must be heralds of reconciliation and that means we must be peacemakers. Those who preach the Gospel must work to establish the kingdom among men [and women]. It means that the Church and the individual Christian are committed to reconcile those at variance, to heal those injustices and inequalities that breed bitterness and conflict, to witness at all times to the brotherhood [and sisterhood] of [human beings]. We have to bring to the world Christ, its peace.

Basil Hume

O God,
From whom on different paths
All of us have come,
To whom on different paths
All of us are going,
Make strong in our hearts what unites us;
Build bridges across all that divides us.
United make us rejoice in our diversity
At one in our witness to that peace
Which you, O God, alone can give.

The Soul of Europe Prayer

Peace moments

Michaela Youngson

I lie on my back on a steep grassy slope,
the sun warming me to my very core,
and watch soft, cotton wool clouds dance by.

In a busy city centre; buses, taxis, vans
dance an argumentative jig.
The shouts and laughter, the swearing and blessing
of the jostling crowd buzz with energy and ordered chaos.

My son's big brown eyes, wide like saucers, awe-struck,
look at his baby sister for the first time,
and a marvellous love is born in a moment.

I hold a smooth, small round pebble
in the palm of my hand, sensing the great age
and gravity of an everyday miracle.

The 'all cried out' feeling, after huge sobs of
relentless grief, no more gasping for air,
just a sense of relief that the storm has passed, for now.

I stand surprisingly still amidst the bustle of a busy art gallery,
breathing in each detail of Monet's *Water Lilies*,
and know that I am changed by this encounter.

The moment, so often too short, of silence
that follows the blessing at the close of worship,
and ends with the chatter that calls to a close
this peace moment.

Moses was keeping the flock of his father-in-law Jethro, the priest of Midian; he led his flock beyond the wilderness, and came to Horeb, the mountain of God. There the angel of the LORD appeared to him in a flame of fire out of a bush; he looked, and the bush was blazing, yet it was not consumed. Then Moses said, 'I must turn aside and look at this great sight, and see why the bush is not burned up.' When the LORD saw that he had turned aside to see, God called to him out of the bush, 'Moses, Moses!' And he said, 'Here I am.' Then he said, 'Come no closer! Remove the sandals from your feet, for the place on which you are standing is holy ground.'

Exodus 3.1-5

The burning bush can be seen as a metaphor for all of creation – it is afire with God. This story illustrates that any place can become a meeting place with God and that God can break into our lives when we least expect it. ... Have you ever had a 'burning bush' experience? Think back on a person or event that gave you a special sense of encounter with the Holy One. How has that experience changed your life? From the habit of imagining the people you see on the street, the trees on the neighbourhood lawns, the place where you spend most of your day, ablaze with fire. What you see with your soul may be truer than what you see with your physical eyes.

The Spiritual Formation Bible (Notes)

God is active in the world and in our lives in many ways. We may feel the mystery of God as we view storm clouds brewing over a blue ocean. We may experience the love of God when we are comforted by a friend. We may be filled with the compassion of God as we attend a conference on the plight of the homeless. We may be blessed by the peace of God during prayer or troubled by the challenges of God as we study the Bible. God comes to us in both our conscious and unconscious experiences, for God is in all of life.

Anne Broyles

It was a dull November day with grey sky and mist. The little brook was scarcely more than a trench to drain the fields, but overhanging it were thorn bushes with a lacework of leafless twigs ...

Laura looked and looked again. A wave of happiness pervaded her being, and although it soon receded, it carried away with it her burden of care. Her first reaction was to laugh aloud at herself. What a fool she had been to make so much of so little. There must be thousands like her who could see no place for themselves in the world, and here she had been, fretting herself and worrying others as if her case were unique. And, deeper down, beneath the surface of her being, was the feeling, rather than the knowledge, that her life's deepest joys would be found in such scenes as this.

Flora Thompson

The beauty of [the star] smote his heart, as he looked up out of the forsaken land, and hope returned to him. For like a shaft, clear and cold, the thought pierced him that in the end the Shadow was only a small and passing thing: there was light and high beauty for ever beyond its reach. ... Now, for a moment, his own fate and even his master's, ceased to trouble him. He crawled back into the brambles and laid himself by Frodo's side, and putting away all fear he cast himself into a deep and untroubled sleep.

J.R.R. Tolkien

Stella had not outgrown her childhood's sensitiveness to colour, scent and sound. The orange glow of the lantern, the warm velvety shadows of the stable, the contented purring of the cats and the breathing of the oxen ... seemed to weave themselves together and make for her a cloak of warm tranquillity. Wrapped in it she lay still, reaching down inside herself for that deep peace in which her being was rooted like a tree. Awareness of that peace gave her the deepest happiness she knew. Sometimes it came, as now, like a deep echo of outward tranquillity ... but she had known it come also in moments of trouble and stress, though it was no more than a touch, gone in a moment yet sufficient in strength to steady one for much longer than its moment of duration.

Elizabeth Goudge

What Monet saw he gave to the world. He saw the infinite beauty of the most ordinary things – a water-lily pond. He saw the dynamism and variability in objects that many of us would regard as generic – lilies and water. But Monet saw that each lily in each season at each time of day was an irrepeatable astonishment. In the particular, in the concrete, in the finite, infinite wonder is beheld.

I will claim this, knowing it is merely an analogy: what Monet saw when he gazed on his water lilies, God must see when beholding creation. Irrepeatable astonishment. Infinity coded in a single leaf. Eternity uttered in the late hour of a summer's afternoon.

Wendy M. Wright

God's holiness is not remote. The God of the Bible is in the here and now. David Jenkins describes God as 'transcendence in the midst'. There is a grubbiness to God's holiness in the sense that his purity and love can be experienced in the dirt, the pain, the everyday of this world. ... It means, secondly, that our holiness needs to be everyday holiness. It is not just about church on a Sunday, or a prayer meeting, or a Bible study. Holiness should pervade the whole of our lives.

David Wilkinson

Finding serenity in change

Peter Middlemiss

The old order changeth, yielding place to new,
  And God fulfils himself in many ways,
Lest one good custom should corrupt the world.

Alfred, Lord Tennyson

Over recent years teachers and those working in the Health Service have regularly had to adjust to new legislation. Every few months commuters have to memorize the latest railway timetable changes. Newly retired people, at last having the spare time to visit their childhood home, find that it has changed beyond all recognition. After living through such experiences some people may feel the final disorientation when they find that something has changed at their local church. New hymn books, new seating, new services can all feel like the last most painful blow if they come from a source that has been identified in the past as a secure safe place. Everyone needs safe places at times and the Church has often been portrayed through history as being a place that resists change. It is not surprising if the beleaguered or stressed disciple sees the Church as a refuge.

The Church is a place where we have all sung so many times a hymn containing the words 'Change and decay in all around I see'. The implication is that change is very much part of decay and that whatever already exists should be defended from attack. So it's not surprising when people inside and outside the Church feel that the eternal changelessness that is often attributed to God should be mirrored in the life of a Church resistant to change.

There are many biblical passages, however, which can lead us to see that change is part of the nature of God. His dealings with Abraham and Moses, for example, suggest that there is quite a bit of movement in God's thinking. The whole of the biblical record helps us see God working in history in a constantly changing world. God is a dynamic innovative power.

The need to be prepared for the inevitability of change is referred to in his book *Holy Living* by the Chaplain to King Charles I, Jeremy Taylor:

> Let us prepare our mind against changes, always expecting them that we may not be surprised when they come: for nothing is so great an enemy to tranquillity and a contented spirit, as the amazement and confusions of unreadiness and inconsideration: and when our fortunes are violently changed, our spirits are unchanged, if they always stood in the suburbs and expectation of sorrows.

Here is a call to everyone to expect change and not to fear the worst when change comes. It is perhaps not surprising that Taylor had such a reaction. During the previous hundred years change was something that his recent ancestors had lived with in the Church. The Reformation had changed the orientation of the Church in England away from Rome. The Authorised Version of the Bible had recently been produced in a style of English that was to be much admired over the next 400 years. (We can wonder whether the translators would have expected their work to have been left unchanged for so long!) Church services were no longer in Latin. Clergy were able to marry and the Monarch had become the Supreme Governor of the Church of England. Change in the Church wasn't, in his experience, to do with decay. The changes brought by the Reformation had brought life to the Church in England. Jeremy Taylor was living in exciting times – even more exciting for his boss the Supreme Governor!

During the last hundred years there have been rapid changes in nearly every aspect of life. Some have had unfortunate knock-on effects that make us worried for the future of life on earth, for social cohesion and for the human spirit. The result of all this is that we can see that more changes are needed if the kingdom that we pray for is to come on earth. We believe that things can get better. In some areas we may feel that change should have happened a long time ago, for example, in the penal system, in world trade agreements, in transport policy and so on. In others we are only just waking up to the issues as new developments in science and technology force us to think the hitherto unthinkable about designer babies or sophisticated methods of checking our identities.

Our local church too might need to embrace change in a far more dramatic way than just reordering the inside of the building or deciding what to sing in it. An emerging church which aims to serve the people may need to do more than Bible studies when sitting on bar stools if it is going to find ways to cope with such a changing world.

The Church will find ways of changing if it really believes that it is an organization that exists for its non-members. We encourage all our fellow citizens to look to the Church for wisdom during difficult times. Shouldn't it come naturally to us to be at the forefront of thinking about change? Not just the inevitability of it, but the ways in which changes can bring us to new avenues of grace!

The approach to change within the Church and the encouragement of change outside have to be rooted in our theology. We see, the more we reflect on the meaning of the 'Universe, Life and Everything', that change is built into the whole system and into the very nature of God. God isn't partially incarnate – being involved in humanity is an all-or-nothing involvement. Since we believe that God is intimately involved in the evolution of our world, we can be confident that change can be good and part of God's creative purpose. We can enjoy challenges to change in our daily lives and work, confident that they are integral to God's call to us. The more we can understand the complexity that is our changing world the more we will be agents for God's purposes.

> God, give us the serenity to accept
>   what cannot be changed;
> Give us the courage to change what
>   should be changed;
> Give us the wisdom to distinguish one
>   from the other.

> Reinhold Niebuhr

'Blessed be the name of God from age to age, for wisdom and power are his. He changes times and seasons, deposes kings and sets up kings; he gives wisdom to the wise and knowledge to those who have understanding. He reveals deep and hidden things; he knows what is in the darkness, and light dwells with him. To you, O God of my ancestors, I give thanks and praise.'

Daniel 2.20-23

To Dame Agnes it was more necessary than ever to be on the alert. 'Be watchful and vigilant, for thine enemy the devil goeth about seeking whom he may devour,' she could have said. 'It's changes, changes, changes,' she mourned. 'It's the climate of the world,' Dame Paula assured her. Pope John had announced, 'We are going to shake off the dust that has collected on the throne of St Peter since the time of Constantine, let in fresh air', and the chill of fresh air, blowing in a closed atmosphere, is always painful; new ideas, new thoughts, new changes were blowing through the monastery, not a fresh breeze as perhaps Pope John had intended, but in gusts, damaging storms.

'Nothing will ever be the same,' said Dame Ursula.

'It's not meant to be,' said Dame Paula.

Rumer Godden

O Lord, in all the changes of this uncertain world,
Grant that we may live in your peace.
Let us not complain in our troubles, nor grow proud in our prosperity.
With calmness of faith, let us rejoice in the goodness of your perfect will,
Through Christ our Lord. Amen.

Jeremy Taylor

Peace comes not by establishing a calm outward setting so much as by inwardly surrendering to whatever the setting.

Hubert van Zeller

It is a good thing to begin each day thanking God for his many blessings in the past. Could any act be more likely to dispel anxiety feelings than to affirm thankfully what God has done for one in the past? For, clearly, God has not changed, and we thus meet the present and face the future confident that he who has seen us through the past will stand by us now.

Leslie Weatherhead

Among Christian people there have been and there still are any different ways of worshipping God. These different ways appeal to different people, and in worship as well as in the rest of life and faith. 'One man's meat is another man's poison,' as the old proverb says. It saddens me that sometimes we easily forget this. We think that because our way of thinking or worshipping is so important to us and right for us that it must be *the* right way, rather than *a* right way. ... At the heart of our faith is a God who is a God of variety and not uniformity, whose generous gift of life produces millions of uniquely different but equally special human beings.

Stephen Dawes

What is needed from each of us today is what I should call an 'expectant faith'. In order to receive the gifts of God, we must *expect* them, be open to them. And in the measure that we are 'expectantly' open to him, the Holy Spirit can accomplish all those wonders that we read about at the beginning of the Church. Each one of us needs that expectant faith.

Michael Ramsey

Men and women who turn their lives over to God will find out that he can make a lot more out of their lives than they can. He will deepen their joys, expand their vision, quicken their minds, strengthen their muscles, lift their spirits, multiply their blessings, increase their opportunities, comfort their souls, raise up friends, and pour out peace. Whoever will lose their life to God will find they have eternal life.

Ezra Taft Benson

God shall be my hope,
My stay, my guide and lantern to my feet.

William Shakespeare

Perhaps we need to look for providence in a different direction. I believe there is evidence that God does break into our affairs just as he chose to break into the life of first-century Palestine in the life, death and resurrection of Jesus. When men and women show remarkable obedience to God which reveals itself not only in courage and faith, but also in outstanding love and compassion, then God can transform their lives into remarkable channels of his love and grace.

Frank Collier

Peace, perfect peace: peace in Isaiah

Michael Thompson

'The peace of God', said St Paul, 'surpasses all understanding' (Philippians 4.7). The apostle suggests that the peace of God, this gift of God that embraces wholeness, health, security and much else, is something that is beyond our ability to fathom and comprehend. Why is this? Is it because we are here confronted by something that is so deeply of God that quite simply earthly imagination and understanding just run out; here is something that is so far beyond our range of human experience, something that when we do experience it we are only, as it were, touching the hem of a garment? Or is it because in both its depths of profundity and in the wideness of its range, it is far beyond our ken? No doubt it is something of all of these, but here I choose to say something about the range, the varieties of peace that are spoken about in just one part of the Bible, the book of Isaiah.

For we may be sure of this. There is a range of meanings of peace in Isaiah. In the first place, there is what we might call the political peace, that particular peace which comes when,

> ... all the boots of the tramping warriors and all the garments rolled in blood shall be burned as fuel for the fire. (Isaiah 9.5)

O happy day when that has taken place! Yet how we still long and pray for that day of peace in our world today. But, we may ask, how can it be? Who or what will bring it about? In Isaiah's vision it is because a most special leader has been given to the nation, a king who will make wise and good political decisions ('Wonderful Counsellor'), who will seem to have near god-like characteristics, at the least being a great gift of God to his people ('Mighty God'), whose concern will not be for himself, either his status or his comforts, but in a most deep and caring way for his people, for he will be truly something of a father to them ('Everlasting Father'), in fact – 'Prince of Peace'. How wonderfully will this one lead those people:

> His authority shall grow continually, and there shall be endless peace for the throne of David and his kingdom. He will establish and uphold it with justice and with righteousness from this time onwards and for evermore. (Isaiah 9.7)

Alas, how frequently it happens that between such visions and the resulting reality so much time must elapse. In so many parts of the world the people wait for the leaders who will put the people first, and who will keep putting them first, who will act with wise and good political judgement, who will strive for justice and freedom and peace on earth.

Then another aspect of peace, and this one is also spoken about in the book of Isaiah: peace with God. For consider: you might – you just might – have the political peace, but even so a person might feel a great emptiness in their life. They might be asking about the life of the world and about life in the world: who is running all this show, who set it going, who made it like it is? Is there anyone out there, around us, and if there is does he or she know me or have any interest in me? And if so, can I reciprocate that relationship? And what happens if I feel that my life has been poor and sinful, not nearly so good as the life in others I meet – for I know how miserable and unworthy my thoughts are. What will God make of me?

And yet for the person who turns to God, there is surely great hope and comfort to be found, depths of the peace of God to be experienced, as expressed in Isaiah 26:

> Those of steadfast mind you keep in peace – in peace because they trust in you. Trust in the Lord for ever, for in the Lord God you have an everlasting rock. (Isaiah 26.3-4)

The peace expressed in the first part of that quotation was rendered in the King James Version of the Bible:

> Thou will keep him in perfect peace, whose mind is stayed on thee: because he trusteth in thee.

For in the Hebrew of this verse the word 'peace' is repeated, and perhaps some emphasis is intended; that is, this person who looks to God in faith and hope can come to know a deep and profound sense of peace. Perhaps indeed, 'perfect peace' may not be an inappropriate translation.

Yet at the same time, how tragic is the opposite situation! For the one who sets themself against God, there is no peace, as the book of Isaiah rings out as if in chorus in a couple of places:

'There is no peace', says the Lord, 'for the wicked.'
(Isaiah 48.22; see also 57.21)

But still, there is a deep peace to be found as we allow ourselves to be led by God. For surely, 'He knows the way he taketh', and when we go in that way, then even though the desert and the difficulties are still there, even though the burdens and the boulders may be upon us and before us, yet nevertheless there can still be that sense of the presence and peace of God overarching and encompassing our lives. This is expressed in another part of Isaiah, in a verse that may originally have been intended to be received by those who were being invited to make a new start in life, by a people for whom great and exciting new possibilities lay before them. Even so, those whose pilgrimage continues may be able to catch the excitement of this moment:

For you shall go out in joy, and be led back in peace; the mountains and the hills before you shall burst into song, and all the trees of the field shall clap their hands. (Isaiah 55.12)

That's when you have found the peace of God for your life. And when you can feel that, yes, you can travel on in a sense of security, peace. Moreover, by something of the same token, how blessed are those who have the good fortune to be the hearers, the receivers of the message of peace. Indeed, what greater ministry can there be in life than to proclaim, by deed or by word, in witness or in worship, something of this peace of God:

> How beautiful upon the mountains are the feet of the messenger who announces peace, who brings good news, who announces salvation, who says to Zion, 'Your God reigns.' (Isaiah 52.7)

And when one of us becomes such a messenger of peace, then another may come to know, or at least to glimpse as if from afar, the 'perfect peace' (Isaiah 26.3) experienced by those whose lives are centred on God. Yet there can be no easy or neat summary of the book of Isaiah's portrayal of peace, much less the Bible's. Rather, the pictures and portrayals of peace in Isaiah are varied and various, some shafts of light coming from a Light too great for us to encounter, at least at present. For, indeed, the peace that the book of Isaiah speaks about is rather like that peace St Paul seeks to proclaim. It is something divine, certainly it comes from the divine side of things, and it is a gift of God to us, something to do with our relationship with him. Perhaps it is really something of God himself, rather as the book of Judges understands, as it tells us about the altar that Gideon built and that he named, 'The Lord is peace' (Judges 6.24). Yes indeed, this is what we are talking about, this we are seeking for ourselves, this we are seeking to point others to:

The peace of God, which surpasses all understanding, will guard your hearts and minds in Christ Jesus. (Philippians 4.7)

The LORD bless you and keep you;
the LORD make his face to shine upon you
    and be gracious to you;
the LORD lift up his countenance upon you,
    and give you peace.

Numbers 6.24-26

It is with wisdom, love, power and serenity that God knows and cares and rules throughout his universal domain. We speak about each attribute in turn, but each time with the rest in view. For it is in the expression of his love, made effective by his power and arising from his serenity, that God is seen to be wise. It is because he is wise and powerful and serene in his loving that we can entrust ourselves to him with a love responding to his own. We look to his power with confidence and hope because the power of God is the practice of wisdom and love grounded in serenity. We acknowledge his serenity with thanksgiving, for if his wisdom, love and power were not conceived in peace and joy they would not bring to the realm of God the full joy and peace which he promises.

From *A Declaration of Faith*

O gracious and holy Father,
give us wisdom to perceive thee,
intelligence to understand thee,
diligence to seek thee,
patience to wait for thee,
eyes to behold thee,
a heart to meditate upon thee,
and a life to proclaim thee;
through the power of the Spirit
of Jesus Christ our Lord.

St Benedict

There is a passage which touches your need. 'For the Eternal … will not let you go.' Faith is not merely your holding on to God – it is God holding on to you. As Walt Whitman puts it, 'Not until the sun refuses to shine, do I refuse you.' Then keep saying to your soul, 'In quietness and confidence shall be your strength' (Isaiah 30.15).

E. Stanley Jones

Ultimately we have just one moral duty: to reclaim large areas of peace in ourselves, more and more peace, and to reflect it towards others. And the more peace there is in *us*, the more peace there will be in our troubled world.

Etty Hillesum

In the castle of my soul there is a little postern gate
Where, when I enter, I am in the presence of God.
In a moment, in a turning of a thought,
I am where God is.
When I meet God there, all life gains a new meaning,
Small things become great, and great things small,
Lowly and despised things are shot through with glory.

My troubles seem but the pebbles of the road,
My joys seem like the everlasting hills,
All my fever is gone in the great peace of God,
And I pass through the door from Time into Eternity.

Walter Rauschenbusch

The prophets of ancient Israel were the first to think globally, to conceive of a God transcending place and national boundaries and of humanity as a single moral community linked by a covenant of mutual responsibility (the covenant with Noah after the Flood). Equally, they were the first to conceive of society as a place where 'justice rolls down like water and righteousness like a never-ending stream' and of a future in which war had been abolished and peoples lived together in peace. Those insights and aspirations have lost none of their power.

Jonathan Sacks

A score of years ago a friend placed in my hand a little book which became one of the turning points of my life. It was called *True Peace.* It was a medieval message, and it had but one thought, which was this – that God was waiting in the depths of my being to talk to me if only I would get still enough to hear his voice.

I thought this would be a very easy matter, and so I began to get still. But I had no sooner commenced than a perfect pandemonium of voices reached my ears, a thousand clamouring notes from without and within, until I could hear nothing but their noise and din. It seemed necessary for me to listen to some of them, but God said, 'Be still, and know that I am God.' Then came the conflict of thoughts for the morrow, and its duties and cares; but God said, 'Be still.'

And as I listened, and slowly learned to obey, and shut my ears to every sound, I found, after a while, that when the other voices ceased, or I ceased to hear them, there was a still, small voice in the depths of my being that began to speak with an inexpressible tenderness, power and comfort. As I listened, it became to me the voice of prayer, and the voice of wisdom, and the voice of duty, and I did not need to think so hard, or pray so hard, or trust so hard, but that 'still small voice' of the Holy Spirit in my heart was God's prayer in my secret soul, was God's answer to all questions, was God's life and strength for soul and body, and became the substance of all knowledge, and all prayer, and all blessing; for it was the living God himself as my life and my all.

John Edward Southall

Contributors

Margaret Cundiff is an Anglican priest, the Associate Minister at St James Church, Selby. She is also part of the ecumenical team at the church in the village of Camblesforth. Margaret is the author of 14 books, and is a regular column writer and broadcaster. She chairs Christians in Communication based in York, and is a well-known conference leader and speaker.

Kenneth G. Greet is a Methodist minister. He was for 17 years the Secretary of the Christian Citizenship Department of the Methodist Church, and for 13 years was Secretary of the Conference. He was President in 1980-81. Dr Greet has broadcast regularly on radio and TV, and is the author of a number of books. He is currently much involved in the peace movement, and is President of the Methodist Peace Fellowship.

Harriet Harris is Chaplain at Wadham College, Oxford, and Assistant Priest of the University Church. She teaches Modern Theology and Philosophy of Religion for the Theology Faculty in Oxford. Her books include *Fundamentalism and Evangelicals* (OUP 1998), *Faith Without Hostages* (SPCK 2002) and, ed. with Jane Shaw, *The Call for Women Bishops* (SPCK 2004).

Donald Macaskill is a freelance trainer and consultant working in the field of equality and diversity. Formerly he taught theology in Scotland and has been a regular contributor to poetry collections. Some of his work can be seen at www.donaldmacaskill.com

Peter Middlemiss is Warden of Holland House Retreat, Conference and Laity Centre in the village of Cropthorne, Worcestershire. He is Chair of the Retreat Association and President of the Ecumenical Association of Academies and Laity Centres in Europe. He has just completed 15 years' membership of the General Synod of the Church of England, and has recently been appointed Honorary Lay Canon of Worcester Cathedral.

Philip J. Morse is the Superintendent Minister of the Exmouth & Budleigh Salterton Circuit and the District Candidates' Secretary of the Plymouth & Exeter District of the Methodist Church. He sends the occasional 'Postcard' to the *Methodist Recorder*. His three favourite places on God's earth are his native Gloucestershire, Le Mans, and Chartres Cathedral (but not necessarily in that order).

John Morrow is a retired minister in the Presbyterian Church in Ireland. He was a member of the Iona Community from 1958-71; a founder member of the Corrymeela Community (1968) and leader of the Community from 1980-93. He has served as a parish minister, in university chaplaincy and as a lecturer at the Irish School of Economics.

Sheila O'Hara entered the International Congregation: Sisters La Sainte Union des Sacres Coeurs in 1940. She has worked in education in both secondary schools and in higher education, and for 18 years has co-ordinated the work of the Peace and Justice Centre in Wrexham. Her interests include the promotion of inter-faith and ecumenical relationships, and she is an active member of CAFOD.

David Painter is a priest of the Church of England, and ministered for 20 years in South London before moving in 2000 to become the Archdeacon of Oakham. In this capacity he is responsible for an area covering the county of Rutland, half of Northamptonshire and the City of Peterborough; he is also a Canon of Peterborough Cathedral.

Chris Polhill is one of the first women priests in the Church of England and currently works in the Lichfield diocese as a member of a team ministry. Chris chairs the Spirituality Team in the diocese, and has trained in Oxford and London to offer spiritual companionship. Chris is also a member of the Iona Community.

Peter Selby is Bishop of Worcester and Bishop to H.M. Prisons. He is author of *Grace and Mortgage: The Language of faith, and the Debt of the World* (Darton, Longman & Todd 1997).

Cecily Taylor's hymn and song lyrics appear in various collections of Stainer & Bell, and in some international hymn books. Her poems have been published in many poetry magazines and anthologies across the denominational spectrum. Formerly a teacher, Cecily has worked since in community relations and with the Quaker Social Justice Committee on human rights.

Michael Thompson is shortly to retire from his position as Superintendent Minister of the Bishop Auckland Circuit of the Methodist Church. He is the author of *I Have Heard Your Prayer*, *The Old Testament and Prayer* (Epworth Press 1996).

Andrew White is the Director of the International Centre for Reconciliation, Residentiary Canon of Coventry Cathedral and Eric Lane Fellow at Clare College, Cambridge. He also served as the Archbishop of Canterbury's Special Representative to the Middle East and continues to be the Director of the Alexandria Track of the Middle East Peace Process. He is a regular visitor to Iraq where he has worked with both the political and religious leadership. He is the author of *Iraq: People of Promise, Land of Despair* (Sovereign World 2003).

Michaela Youngson is a Methodist minister who, having served for nine years in churches in Lancashire, is now the Secretary for Pastoral Care and Spirituality in the Methodist Church. She is the author of *Making the Colours Sing* (Inspire 2005).

Acknowledgements

Inspire gratefully acknowledges the use of copyright items. Every effort has been made to trace copyright owners, but where we have been unsuccessful we would welcome information which would enable us to make appropriate acknowledgement in any reprint.

Scripture quotations are from the New Revised Standard Version of the Bible, (Anglicized Edition) © 1989, 1995 by the Division of Christian Education of the National Council of Churches of Christ in the United States of America. Used by permission. All rights reserved.

Page

3   Joyce Rupp, *The Cosmic Dance*, Orbis Books 2002. Used by permission.

10   David Adam, *The Open Gate*, by permission of SPCK.

13   Lloyd C. Douglas, *The Big Fisherman*, Pan Books 1972.

19   Dietrich Bonhoeffer, *The Cost of Discipleship*, SCM Press.

20   Wayne Dosick, *Soul Judaism: Dancing with God in a New Era*, Jewish Lights Publishing.

20   Bede, *The Ecclesiastical History of the English People*, ed. Bertram Colgrave, R.A.B. Mynors, OUP 1969.

21   Ann Bird, *Living in Communion*, MPH 1998.

21   J. Neville Ward, *Beyond Tomorrow*, Epworth Press.

25   John Baillie, *A Diary of Private Prayer,* Charles Scribners Sons 1949.

25   Michel Quoist, *With Open Heart*, tr. Colette Copeland, Gill & Macmillan 1983.

27   Evelyn Underhill, *Meditations and Prayers*, Longmans, Green 1949.

27   W. Paul Jones, 'The Heresy of Peace', *Weavings*, Nov-Dec 1998, The Upper Room.

28   Ladislaus Boros, *God is With Us*, Search Press Ltd, in Elizabeth Goudge, *A Book of Faith*, Hodder & Stoughton 1976.

37   Martin Luther King, *The Words of Martin Luther King*, selected by Coretta Scott King, Collins 1986.

37   Bede Griffiths OSB, *The Universal Christ*, ed. Peter Spink, Darton, Longmann & Todd 1993.

45   Flora Slosson Wuellner, *Enter by the Gate*, Upper Room Books 2004.

46   Oscar Romero, *The Violence of Love – The Words of Oscar Romero*, Collins.

46   Jean Vanier, *The Broken Body*, Darton, Longman & Todd.

47   E. Glenn Hinson, 'On Being God's Pencil', *Weavings*, Nov-Dec 1998, The Upper Room.

53   Anne Doyle, *Seasons with the Spirit*, CTBI 2002. Permission applied for.

54   Amy Carmichael, from *Mountain Breezes*, copyright © 1999, The Dohnavur Fellowship. Used by permission.

54   William Sykes, *Visions of Grace*, BRF 1997.

55   Thomas R. Hawkins, *A Life that becomes the Gospel*, Upper Room Books 1992.

56   Perran Gay, 'Father God, your love surrounds us', written as a hymn for the Decade of Evangelism. Used by permission of the author.

65   'I believe', World Council of Churches 1985 from *Confessing our Faith Around the World IV. South America 1985: Confession of Faith from a Service for Human Rights*, Chile, Nov. 1978, WCC Geneva. Permission applied for.

68   Leslie Griffiths, *Letters Home*, Foundery Press.

71   Dorothy Wordsworth, *Grasmere Journal* in *The Lake District, An Anthology*, comp. Norman Nicholson, Penguin Books 1977.

73   Anthony Hulbert, *Contours of God*, The Canterbury Press 1995.

74   Edith Holden, *The Country Diary of an Edwardian Lady*, Michael Joseph 1977.

74 Alison Uttley, *The Country Child*, Puffin Books 1977.

81 Brian Wren, 'Say "No" to Peace', © 1986, Stainer & Bell Ltd.

83 Gustavo Gutierrez, 'Compassion and Commitment', *Weavings*, Nov-Dec 1990, The Upper Room.

91 William Barclay, *The Gospel of John*, St Andrew Press 1974.

92 Luigi Santucci, *Wrestling with Christ*, Fontana Books 1974.

99 John Johansen-Berg, *Prayers for Today's World*, Epworth Press.

100 Gordon Macdonald, *Ordering your Private World*, Highland Books 1990.

100 Olive Wyon, *On the Way*, SCM Press 1958.

101 Dorothee Soelle, *Against the Wind, Memoir of a Radical Christian*, Fortress Press 1999.

102 Leslie J. Tizard, *Facing Life and Death*, George Allen and Unwin 1959.

107 Jim Forest, *The Ladder of the Beatitudes*, Orbis Books 1999.

108 Janet Lees, 'In the heat of memory', *Textures of Tomorrow*, URC 1986, and by permission of the author.

109 Eric Gallagher, in Dennis Cooke, *Peacemaker, the life and work of Eric Gallagher*, MPH 2005.

109 Prayer from CTBI material for the Queen's Golden Jubilee 2002, in *Beyond our Tears*, CTBI 2004. Permission applied for.

110 Basil Hume, *To be a Pilgrim: A Spiritual Notebook*, St Paul Publications, Triangle SPCK 1999.

113 *The Spiritual Formation Bible* (Notes), Upper Room Books/The Zondervan Corporation.

114 Anne Broyles, *Journalling*, Upper Room Books 1999.

114 Flora Thompson, *Lark Rise to Candleford*, Penguin Modern Classics 1977.

115 J.R.R. Tolkien, *The Lord of the Rings*, HarperCollins Publishers 1991.

115 Elizabeth Goudge, *Gentian Hill*, Hodder & Stoughton 1950.

116 Wendy M. Wright, *The Time Between, Cycles and Rhythms in Ordinary Time*, Upper Room Books 1999.

116 David Wilkinson, *A Holiness of the Heart*, Monarch Books 2000.

122 Rumer Godden, *In this House of Brede*, Pan Books 1970.

123 Leslie Weatherhead, *Prescription for Anxiety*, Hodder & Stoughton 1970.

124 Stephen Dawes, *Desert Island Hymns: Faith which sings with heart and mind*, Southleigh Publications 1996.

124 Michael Ramsey, Leon Joseph Cardinal Suenens, *Come, Holy Spirit,* Darton, Longman & Todd 1977.

125 Frank Collier, *Strangers & Pilgrims*, Foundery Press 1996.

132 *A Declaration of Faith*, The Congregational Church in England and Wales 1967.

134 Jonathan Sacks, *The Dignity of Difference*, Continuum 2003.